SCOTT ALEXANDER KING

WORLD ANIMAL DREAMING
ORACLE CARDS

ILLUSTRATED BY KAREN BRANCHFLOWER

www.rockpoolpublishing.com.au

A Rockpool card set
PO Box 252
Summer Hill
NSW 2130
Australia
www.rockpoolpublishing.com.au
www.facebook.com/RockpoolPublishing

First published in 2012
Copyright text © Scott Alexander King
Copyright illustrations © Karen Branchflower

ISBN 9781921878787

All rights reserved. No part of this publication may be reproduced, stored in a retrieval system, or transmitted in any form or by any means, electronic, mechanical, photocopying, recording or otherwise, without the prior written permission of the publisher.

Designed by Liz Seymour
Typesetting by Lisa Shillan
Editing by Karen Tait
Printed in China

10 9 8 7 6 5 4 3 2

For Patrick

Walk with me! The time has come for you to learn of many things.
Walk with me and we will go over the seas to distant lands.
Walk with me, I sing the songs of ancient kin; our animals.
Walk with me, the message says, we don't have long to feel again.
Walk with me and I will talk of how it is and what shall be.
  Patricia Hullan, 2011

CONTENTS

ACKNOWLEDGMENTS 1
INTRODUCTION 2
ABOUT THE WORLD ANIMAL SPIRITS 8
   What are the animals telling us? 10
HOW TO READ THE WORLD ANIMAL
DREAMING ORACLE CARDS 18
   The World Animal Dreaming Card Spreads 22
      The Basic Three Card Spread 22
      The Big Five Spread 24
      The World Animal Dreaming Totem Spread 28
      The Ancestor Spread 34
CARD INTERPRETATIONS 37
EAST / AIR / GOLDEN YELLOW 39
   Bald Eagle – Oneness 40
   Antelope – Radiance 42
   Lion – Languor 44
   Rhinoceros – Staying Power 46
   Cheetah – Vigour 48
   Pheasant – Lovers 50
   Horned Owl – Warning 52
   Butterfly – Transformation 54
   Horse – Personal Power 56
   Otter – Playfulness 58
   Ghost Bat – Rebirth 60
   Polar Bear – Brotherhood 62
NORTH / FIRE / OCHRE RED 65
   Meerkat – Dependability 66
   Wildebeest – The Victim 68

- Zebra – Individuality 70
- Tiger – Cowardice 72
- Ant – Strength 74
- Coyote – The Joker 76
- Bee – Potential 78
- Gorilla – Essence 80
- Grey Wolf – The Pathfinder 82
- Skunk – Compromise 84
- Crocodile – Creative Force 86

WEST / WATER / DARK BLUE 89
- Hippopotamus – Volatility 90
- Giraffe – Intersection 92
- Asiatic Black Bear – The Prostitute 94
- Giant Panda – Sorrow 96
- Red Panda – Compassion 98
- Black Bear – Introspection 100
- Crow – Law 102
- Dolphin – Breath 104
- Jaguar – Impeccability 106
- Spider – The Weaver 108
- Whale – Ground Signatures 110

SOUTH / EARTH / LEAF GREEN 113
- African Elephant – Commitment 114
- Ostrich – Grounding 116
- Chimpanzee – Ascension 118
- Orang–utan – Man of the Forest 120
- Bison – Sacred Prayer 122
- Puma – Leadership 124
- Dog – Loyalty 126
- Rabbit – Fertility 128
- Jackal – Death 130
- Turkey – Shared Blessings 132
- Moose – Durability 134

ACKNOWLEDGMENTS

I would like to offer a heart-felt thank you to Rockpool Publishing. I truly appreciate how patient and generous you are as people and how ethical and honest you are as a company.

I would also like to thank my dear friend Karen Branchflower for her powerful illustrations and her dedication to making this deck of oracle cards just as beautiful as its sister set, the (all-Australian) *Animal Dreaming Oracle Cards*.

I would like to send my love and thanks to my Animal Dreaming State Reps: Ruth Lennie, Jeanette Cochrane, Jo Kinnear, Nicky Marsden and Elise Brooks, for your love, support and commitment to all things Animal Dreaming. Without your support, my sisters, life would be less than perfect.

I would like to acknowledge my deep love and respect for our beautiful Earth Mother and all the world's animals, without which I would have little reason to get up in the morning: Ever since I was a child, you've watched over me, guided me and offered me experience, wisdom, healing and abundance. You've never turned your back on me, nor have you ever broken a promise, turned me away, stolen from me or mocked me in any way. You've always been there for me, and by offering this beautiful deck of oracle cards, I hope you realise that I will always be there for you.

And most importantly I would like to thank my beautiful wife, Trudy, and my three amazing children, Rosie, Kaleb and Oskar for believing in me with all their hearts. I love you more than life itself.

INTRODUCTION

I've had many animals come into my life over the years. Some have simply turned up on my doorstep, others have been given to me and some I have bought. I have always surrounded myself with animals and have always felt much more comfortable in their company than I have ever felt with people. To name just a few of the creatures that have shared my home, there have been: Horses and Ponies, Alpacas, Cattle, Sheep, Goats, Pigs, Geese, Turkeys, Chickens, Ducks, Guineafowl, Peacocks, Rabbits, Guinea-pigs, Possums, Lizards, Ferrets, Rats and Mice, Bats, Pigeons, Doves, Parrots, Lorikeets and Parakeets, Cockatoos, Galahs, Partridges, Quail, Pheasants, Finches and Canaries, Tortoises, Frogs, Dogs and Cats. I've loved them all ... but the ones that have had the biggest impact on my life were the two hand-tamed Foxes (a male and a female) that grew up alongside my daughter, Rosie. She would wrap them up tightly in towels and carry them around like babies. Todd (named after the Fox in the 1981 Disney animated feature, *The Fox and the Hound*) came into my life first. He delivered as a tiny cub to a lady's house in the Yarra Valley, Victoria in a load of compost she had ordered from the local garden supply centre. She took him to her vet and from the vet he came to live with me. The other Fox, a near-adult female, came to me via a friend who had found her sniffing around his rubbish bin. She wore a red collar, so it was obvious that someone else had already raised her from a cub. As she was skinny and timid, it was also obvious that she had been loose for some time and that she didn't know how to fend for herself. I called her Moonlight, because it was in the moonlight that she was found. Those Foxes were so magickal, so proud and unapologetic. They loved to frolic, sing, yap and play. They groomed their tails constantly and slept all rolled up together in a warm little ball. They never bit or nipped, despite the fact that they hated being handled and they never caused an ounce of trouble. I loved them both very much. I would call upon them energetically when I engaged in ritual or ceremony and I felt their spirit with me while I worked or went about my daily chores. I knew they were with me when I slept and I always knew when they wanted to be fed or watered because I would hear their call in my heart. But despite this close bond, I also felt their forever-wild nature and their strong desire to be free. The Foxes weren't tame. They weren't mine. They were their own beings. And it was for this reason that I knew in my heart that neither would ever become my 'familiar'. Not in the truest sense of the word at least.

While I understand what it means to have one now, my longing to have a *physical* familiar has been with me since I was very young. Not a pet that I would have to take places in a basket or on a lead, but a TRUE familiar; an animal friend that would accompany me (by choice) wherever I went, helping me with my chores and school work. How wonderful would it be to have a constant ally, who loved you for who you are and was willing to lend a hand no matter what? I desperately wanted to know what it was like. I would ask the animals I came across to be my familiar. I asked the Rabbits that ran about in the fields, the Foxes that skulked in the forest, the Frogs that sat proudly on the edge of our creek, but none of them seemed to understand a word I was saying. I called to the Ravens and the Owls, the Horses and the Cows, but none of them took any notice of me. I was so confused and I couldn't figure out why the notion of familiars was 'invented' if it was impossible to get the animals to take the idea seriously! I offered the animals gifts of food and made them little houses. I even offered to brush them but they all ignored me! And then it dawned on me. Perhaps I wasn't supposed to find my familiar at all. Perhaps I was supposed to wait for them to approach me; to come to me with the idea? So I sat and waited ... and waited ... and waited! And then I forgot to wait. And then I just plain forgot!

And then out of the blue I found my familiar; a beautiful white Barn Owl with caramel-coloured wings, back and neck, huge wise eyes, strong claws and a powerful beak. Apparently she had always been with me, but because I had been looking for her with my physical eyes, I couldn't see her! My familiar had found me on the etheric plane and it was only with my 'subtle' vision that I could see her. By looking through my third eye rather than my two 'actual' eyes, I could see her clearly. And even to this day, she continues to go everywhere I go. I call upon my Barn Owl when I'm meditating, writing, pondering or offering readings and healings. She's with me when I go grocery shopping, preparing dinner for my family, feeding my animals or gardening. In fact, she's with me all the time, even when I'm sleeping! My Barn Owl has become my protector and guide, my muse, friend and confidant. She keeps me company, balanced and in peace. She warns me of danger and shows me where to find light whenever I find myself lost or confused. She gives me advice and answers my questions. She offers me stronger connection to my guides and to Spirit, assisting me in my journeys, manifestations and visualisations. But most of all, she maintains my integrity by warning me when I'm being lied to and when I need to keep my mouth shut so that silence, truth and wisdom may prevail.

The really silly thing is, long before the Barn Owl made herself known to me, I remember having a Black Cat follow me everywhere I went – a regular black 'moggy'; nothing at all special to look at or particular in any way. I honestly thought the Cat was real and I would say to my parents, 'The Cat's here again' and they would just say, 'Is it?' They never asked why they couldn't see it and would smile in a dismissive way. I would see it at school. I would feel it sitting on the end of my bed, purring loudly, at night. I would be in the shower and I would see it sitting on the vanity basin. I would come home from school and it would be, sitting in the lounge room waiting for me (it would sometimes peer around the corner and smile at me). In fact, I thought everybody could see it because no one questioned me or made any comments when I spoke of it.

But what really made me stop and wonder was when I was about 15, the Cat stood up on its back legs and morphed into my grandfather! It happened very quickly, but I knew at that moment that he had been watching over me my entire childhood. And then he spoke to me and I could tell by his tone when he said, 'You'll be alright' that he meant for me nothing but love.

As a small child, I didn't think of animals as belonging to any one particular continent, culture or nation. I never thought, 'Because I'm an Aussie, I need to have an Aussie animal as my favourite'. I loved them all equally and as brothers and sisters. I didn't care where they came from or what gods or goddesses they were associated with. They are native or indigenous to our beautiful planet, and it's to this planet that we all belong, so why should it be any different with animals? We all belong to one global tribe, making it possible for us to have totems, animal guides and power animals from anywhere in the world. If I was to look at what it means for me to be 'Australian', I would learn that my original family blood-line extends from Scotland to North America, making the animals native or indigenous to those areas just as relevant to me on a totemic level as the many beautiful and unique animals I share my home with.

As most people who own this deck will know, I first became known for my work with the medicine or 'Dreaming' of the Australian animals. My first book, *Animal Dreaming*, and the inspiration-based deck that followed, the *Animal Dreaming Oracle Cards*, were (and still are) the two publications that anchored my work here in Australia and overseas. The *Animal Dreaming Oracle Cards* in particular, attracted a lot of positive attention because not for the longest time had there been an oracle deck dedicated just to the messages and medicine wisdom of the Australian animals.

The main difference between this new 'world' deck and the original is that this deck showcases animals globally while the *Animal Dreaming Oracle Cards* offers the messages of animals synonymous with Australia. This deck is the exotic 'sister-deck' to my *Animal Dreaming Oracle Cards* and can be used separately to, or in harmony with it. One will support the other, no matter how the cards are used or in which order they're laid out. I think they'll work very well together, not just because they are both animal decks written by the same author and illustrated by the same artist, but because they're sisters born from the same dream instilled with the one vision and joint purpose.

When I first consciously began my spiritual journey, I used to read both the *Medicine Cards* and the *Sacred Path Cards* by Jamie Sams and David Carson for guidance and insight. I used to read them separately, but I also loved to read them combined, by assembling a spread using the Medicine Cards before laying the Sacred Path Cards over the top to deepen the messages of the animals, or the other way around to enhance the messages of the Sacred Path Cards by asking the animals for their clarifying wisdom.

ABOUT THE WORLD ANIMAL SPIRITS

With the creation of the *World Animal Dreaming Oracle Cards* came the desire to foster within you, the seeker, a deeper appreciation of the animals that you have bonded with, or that you may sense spiritually, with yourself or others. I hope to broaden the understanding of the animals that physically share this planet with you too, by endorsing them as more than just pets or playthings. The animals, to me, are and always have been sacred messengers of Spirit and I am thrilled to have been given this opportunity to share the symbolisms that I have grown to celebrate as my personal connection to Spirit.

I've seen animals with people since I was a kid. Not in the physical sense (although for many years, I didn't know they weren't 'really there'), but rather in the astral, the in-between space between our world and the realms of Spirit. Whenever I meet someone for the first time, I can clearly see an animal with them, standing either to their left or right or sitting on their shoulder. The animals tell me things about the people: about their lives, their hobbies, their hopes and fears. I hear their voices as feelings, like memories placed in my mind that I know aren't mine. Their mere presence offers insight, too – messages based on the wisdom I have come to know and understand; symbolic meanings inspired by the way they would relate and interact with each other and their natural environment in the tangible world. The animals seem to change each time I see the person thereafter. It's as if the animal represents where the person is at emotionally, physically or spiritually at that time, its energy mirroring that of the person it shadows. Sometimes these animals manifest as loved ones in Spirit – but not in the way you'd expect to see them. When I see someone's passed-over loved one, for example, they always show themselves to me in an animal form; an animal archetype that best captures their character, their spirit, and their true essence. I might see your dad as a Bear; your son as a Monkey or your aunty as a Snow Leopard. Depending on the animals I see, I am also able to determine whether or not the person I see them with is grieving, in pain or suffering from illness. I am also able to tell other stuff about your life too ... whether or not your son is likely to find himself in trouble with the law, for example, or if your house will sell in time. I can explain the best way to reach your potential, or to find that perfect job – all because I have the ability to access the realms of Spirit.

People ask me, 'Are they totems, power animals, familiars, archetypes or what?' Generally, I don't give an answer, and that's mainly because I don't have one to give! I simply don't know. I've tried to explain them away as being nothing more than the aura in animalistic form or a totemic manifestation of the chakras working predominantly with the people they accompany ... but none of these explanations have ever really felt 'right'. After reading Patrick Harpur's book, however, *The Philosopher's Secret Fire*, I wondered if the 'animals' I'd been seeing were in fact daimons – beings that walk with each and every one of us, offering insight, clarity, direction and purpose. The description given by Harpur helped explain why the animals changed form; why sometimes I referred to them as 'he' one day, and 'she' the next; why sometimes they felt like 'mother' energy, and then other times, more like the 'father'. Perhaps these animals are 'daimons' and perhaps I am a 'daimonic man'. One thing I can say for certain is that the animals I see ARE contradictory. They DO change shape and gender. Sometimes they DO change shape, while retaining the same energy. They CAN be the same 'entity', while appearing as another or in another form. They DO appear to be physical and non-physical at the same time. And they DO offer insight, direction and clarity and at times, DO appear as Angels. For years I have been visited by a Black Jaguar that has crystal-blue eyes, and for years I've seen an apple-green Tree Snake. I didn't take much notice because it wasn't out of the ordinary for me to see animals in or around my home. And then it struck me … Jaguars don't normally have blue eyes. So, you can imagine my surprise when I asked the Jaguar one day, 'Who are you?' to hear his straightforward reply … 'Michael'. The surprises continued when the Tree Snake told me his name was 'Raphael'.

WHAT ARE THE ANIMALS TELLING US?

We need to first break this massive 'family' into smaller categories to better understand the energies that we're working with. Instead of looking at them as just 'animals', let's look at them as 'mammals', 'birds', 'aquatics', 'insects' and 'reptiles':

- **Mammals**: Ruled by the earth element, like us, mammals are all very emotional beings. But, unlike us, the mammals we find in the animal kingdom (those that are 'non-human') do not project their emotions. They don't assume that others are feeling the same way they are at any given time like we do. For example, we feel guilty when we leave our Dog at home by herself because we assume she will miss us and get lonely. We believe that's how the Dog is feeling because that's how we would feel if we were left at home alone. The Dog is unlikely to feel the loneliness we project. Nevertheless, all mammals represent our emotional self, so any mammal that we witness either in dreams, in the flesh or symbolically (on T-shirts, on the TV or on a billboard, etc) are all offering messages associated with our emotional self or the emotions generically.

- **Birds**: Whether they fly or not (penguins, ostrich, rhea, emus and kiwis can't fly, for example), birds are all associated with the mind, the mental self and 'the head'. Ruled by the element Air, birds are not bound by the same emotions as mammals are. They're able to 'detach' themselves to some degree from the emotional pool that seems to hinder humanity's ability to grow and prosper as much as it seems to enrich it; to see the bigger picture from a broader perspective. Birds teach us to see what needs to be done, when it needs to be done by and how, without allowing ourselves to invest in the 'what ifs?' or to be burdened by emotions that may be triggered in the process. Birds can also be seen as symbols of the Soul. They reflect our connection to the heavenly realms and Spirit and remind us to strive for higher levels of consciousness and awareness, by offering the ability to raise ourselves above perceived obstacles.

- **Aquatics**: Ruled by the element water all creatures that call the oceans, streams, lakes, rivers, dams and billabongs home are associated with intuition; the ability to tap into our inner knowing and to find answers to questions buried deep within. They speak of meditation, contemplation and introspection and they allow us to tune into our inner voice and to hear what our higher self has to say. Aquatics aren't necessarily fish though; some are mammals or birds, while others are reptilians. It's important, when dealing with an aquatic that isn't a fish, to consider the other factors that make up its being. For example, an Otter is an aquatic mammal and could be asking us to intuitively listen to how we feel or how our actions are affecting someone emotionally. Pelicans are aquatic birds and could be asking us to intuitively override what our mind may be asking us to do and to listen to our gut or 'animal instinct' when it comes to some decision we need to make. There's no right or wrong way to consult the animals, but by simply making an effort to understand them, we're a heck of a lot closer to finding what works for us.

- **Reptiles**: Ruled by the element fire reptiles (Snakes, Lizards, Monitors, Turtles, Tortoises, Crocodiles, etc) all require the heat and warmth of the fiery sun for motivational purposes. They look to the heat for energy and symbolically channel it into passion, desire, drive, adventure, enthusiasm, excitement, ambition and will. They teach us to explore our ability to be still while the masculine energy of the sun motivates and inspires us. Instead of acting irrationally and making rushed decisions, though, reptile energy allows us to sit, dream and envision the future. Once we know what we want our future to look, feel, taste, sound and smell like, the reptile energy encourages us to move forward in a practical, purposeful, passionate way.

- **Insects and Arachnids**: While Spiders, Ticks, Scorpions and the like aren't insects (they're all arachnids), they tend to be placed in the same basket as insects when it comes to looking at them from a medicine point of view. And this is because, being that they're ruled by the fifth element – spirit, they journey with us into our inner worlds, the spiritual realms hidden deep in our psych. From the art of stillness to the wonder of personal and spiritual transformation, insects speak of all aspects of the inner self and the connection we all share with Spirit.

Once we've considered what these categories might mean to us on a symbolic level, we need to take an even closer look at how they come into our life and why; whether they're endangered, dead, alive or representational of animals we love or fear. All these factors mean something and they all act as powerful ways to explore the deeper meaning of the appearance of our animal brothers and sisters.

- When you next experience an animal in an unusual setting or circumstances (or the 'meeting' seems more than just a chance encounter), consider that the animal in question has been 'sent to you' by your Earth Mother in response to a question or issue plaguing your mind. What were you thinking about when you encountered the animal? Consider this and then look at the animal's 'medicine'. Its message will most certainly 'answer' your 'question' with a clarity and accuracy that may surprise you!

- Sometimes they will appear physically or they may appear in abstract ways. The secret lies in knowing where to look and how to integrate their messages into your life. When you find yourself pondering a particular problem and you find yourself stuck as to what to do, simply widen your vision to the animals that may be trying to make themselves known to you in obscure ways. Once you see a pattern (the same animal appearing over and over) consider the 'meaning' of that animal's symbology and consider that as a possible 'answer' to your question. The Parrot on the side of the Arnott's Truck, for example, may be encouraging you to talk further about a situation; the Rhino logo on a kid's T-shirt may be suggesting you push forward anyway; while the 'Tiger in your Tank' bumper sticker may be suggesting the need for you to find the courage to face the issue in front of you and to stop beating around the bush. If you find yourself 'bombarded' with a particular animal; seeing it over and over and you want to know what that animal is trying to tell you, simply recall what you were thinking about at the time of the encounters and you may be surprised to find it was the same issue each time. The animal 'bothering' you holds insight into how you might handle / resolve the issue at hand.

- Seeing an animal dead on the side of the road is a significant event most of us overlook. While seeing a live animal may offer insight into what you may have been considering, a dead animal can offer insight into what you've been ignoring or denying. These animals stop us in our tracks and say 'stop pretending not to know ... you have the answer within you but you're ignoring it'.

- Extinction Implications: I believe that if we allow certain animals to slip away into the realms of extinction, the implications for humanity would mean more than the physical loss of another species. Their loss, depending on their symbology, would also herald spiritual repercussions for us as a decline in our potential, perhaps, or the loss of hope, vision and connection to something 'bigger' than our known world.

- An allergy to a particular animal may actually be the physical manifestation of a severe subconscious block set up to save us from ever having to deal with the 'real reason' that lays hidden within the animal's symbolism. An allergy to Cats, for example, may represent the inability to acknowledge sexual abuse or the grief associated with never seeing justice done or the perpetrator never taking responsibility for his or her actions. A fear of ('Pussy') Cats may mean that you lack sexual confidence, suffered from abuse, a neglectful mother, multiple miscarriages, involuntary termination of a pregnancy, etc. A phobia or allergy surrounding Cats could suggest that you've tried unsuccessfully to speak about your sexual issue or have been ignored, not believed, punished or ridiculed for speaking up. It manifests as a hatred of Cats; the one animal (subconsciously) linked to the sexual region of all women; an association that dates back to medieval times.

- The animals we love/admire reflect our strengths and the self-confidence we feel regarding certain aspects of our life. A love of the Wolf, for example, suggests a natural ability to teach, demonstrate and explain. A love of Mountain Lions suggests innate leadership skills, while Cheetahs symbolise a natural athletic ability, Snakes speak of inherent healing skills while Horse suggests a wild streak; an individual who loves being outdoors. To work with the animals we love will see us one day reaching our potential (especially when we similarly 'consult' or consider those that we fear).

- Animals witnessed in dreams offer insight into our subconscious knowing. They open doors to our wild, primal self; that part of our knowing that seems too 'out there' or left of field. They speak to us from our true self, that part of us that still knows the truth about who and what we are, despite the years of reprogramming and indoctrination performed by family, society and 'the system'. To dream of a Dolphin, for example, can offer early warning of an as-yet undetected pregnancy, Snakes can forewarn of a medical problem that, if left undetected, could lead to further complications, while a Kookaburra can ease the fear of continued illness by fore-telling a time of renewed good health and a new beginning.

- Are you a Dog person or a Cat person: a simple question that's easily answered? Not always! Knowing whether you're a 'Cat Person' or a 'Dog Person' (you can only be one or the other) offers (often humorous) insight into your personality and character. Understanding why you do certain things and act in particular ways can all be explained by discovering whether you're a 'Cat Person' or not. Although it does make a difference whether or not you like Cats over Dogs, if you have 'always had Dogs', or if you hate Cats, it doesn't always answer the question of 'what type am I'. They're simply archetypes that determine your character or personality. People who 'once liked Cats' but find themselves now drawn to Dogs (or vice versa), can similarly learn a lot about themselves by seeing this shift as a type of emotional, physical or spiritual transition.

- What about Animal Magick and their role in the art of manifestation? Knowing what animals to 'invoke' or to spiritually call upon to help with a particular situation can spell the difference between success and failure. In similar fashion to how the ancients may have 'danced' a certain animal in ceremony before a hunt to ensure a successful kill, we too can call in the 'Dreaming' or medicine of a certain animal to ensure success on any level. I, for example, always picture myself surrounded by Squirrels and Mice when I go to the bank to get a loan because Squirrels are 'good at saving, hoarding and collecting' while Mice, being nervous and afraid of being eaten, are good with contracts and the associated 'fine print'.

HOW TO READ THE WORLD ANIMAL DREAMING ORACLE CARDS

The *World Animal Dreaming Oracle Cards* have been developed with the energies of the four directions in mind with the traditional correspondences exclusive to each direction determining the animals represented and the wisdom imparted.

EAST: With the Bald Eagle delegated as the 'zero card', representational of Great Spirit, **the first 11 cards** symbolise the lessons of the East, collectively embracing the gifts of intuition, clarity of mind and illumination. The East is governed by the element Air, and is the birthplace of the Sun each day. It is that point in time where we enter the world as a newborn child and the phase that allows us to trust our instinct on things.

NORTH: The next 11 cards harness the energies of the North and the element Fire. The animals represented by these cards cooperatively set about acknowledging the lessons of power, passion and innocence. The energy of the North symbolises the Sun as it sits directly overhead at midday. It represents the teenage years when we know everything, yet nothing at the same time. It is the phase that suggests that if we follow our true life path we would have the potential to live a prosperous, happy and complete life.

WEST: The next 11 cards, charged with the energies of the West and the element of Water, embrace the emotions and the lessons of introspection, contemplation and meditation. Embodying the energies at dusk, the West symbolically represents the phase in life where we find ourselves asking, 'Is this it?', and the resulting choices that present themselves.

SOUTH: The final 11 cards harness the power of midnight, the Earth element and the gifts of maturity and wisdom. The animals that harness the energies of the South demonstrate how far we have come and the experience and acumen afforded us in doing so. This phase suggests we may have achieved all that we could under the circumstances, and to the very best of our abilities.

Some say that there are five elements, with the fifth signifying either Spirit or Love. The energy and the intent imbued within the 45 *World Animal Dreaming Oracle Cards* views the fifth element as being the love and protection sought by those who walk their talk and strive to embrace a spiritual existence. The purpose of the *World Animal Dreaming Oracle Cards* is to assist People in their healing, their purpose and their own personal connection to Spirit. This appreciation, as a portrayal of the fifth element, is imbued throughout the cards as a common perception, and must be sought out in a manner personal to the seeker.

The *World Animal Dreaming Oracle Cards* can be selected individually on a daily basis as points of focus for meditation, affirmation or daily life lessons and incorporated into how one approaches the world, runs one's life or interacts with other people. This method honours the animals in their traditional role as teachers and guides, and as a sacred link to Spirit. By consulting a different card each day we are effectively taking a Walkabout without having to leave the room. We are taking our intent and offering it to Creation by asking Spirit to send us the most appropriate sign or message to assist us with the day's events.

The Walkabout is not just a stroll taken in nature. It is a journey of intent, undertaken with the purpose of communing with Spirit, Creation and Mother Earth. It encourages us to find and honour the silence within so that we may communicate with all of Creation. It is hoped that the walker will find it possible to take their experiences and the significant things they see, hear, smell and touch, as gifts and messages from Spirit, purposefully integrating the wisdom into their life.

Choosing a card embraces the entire process without expecting one to physically walk anywhere. Sitting still with the cards so that one may find the silence within before choosing a card is essential, as it creates a safe place and a sacred connection between you and the energies of Nature represented by the cards.

Alternatively, it is quite acceptable to intuitively create a spread for yourself that captures the essence of what you need from the cards, or to adapt the cards to a traditional spread. The Three Card Spread is a generic option whereby the cards represent past influences, the present, and future potentials that may help clarify your life path. The Celtic Cross Spread is a commonly used spread in other systems and may also be adopted or adapted as a possible alternative. However, the *World Animal*

Dreaming Oracle Cards have been developed to be used in spreads designed especially for their purpose.

Regardless of which spread is used, the interpretations of the cards have been intentionally written to focus only on the positive application. It is intended that should a card appear in a contrary or inverted position, the reader should simply turn the card upright. This has been done with the belief that if the reader's life was free of obstacles and concerns, there should be no need to consult the cards in the first place. To consult the cards indicates a need for clarity, guidance and confirmation. To offer a negative viewpoint is to focus on fear. It threatens to deliver the reader into a place that reinforces low self-esteem and a lack of confidence. It may also negate any feelings of blossoming motivation and optimism. Most people are willing to strive for more and initiate healing when their lessons are approached from a glass half-full perspective rather than half-empty.

THE WORLD ANIMAL DREAMING CARD SPREADS

THE BASIC THREE CARD SPREAD

The Three Card Spread is a quick, easy method of determining the energies moving through your life at any one given time. It offers insight into your past experiences, your present circumstances and your future potential. It helps us remove blocks (typically rooted in past experience) that prevent future movement and growth by helping us to stand purposefully in the now. By addressing the past and integrating the lessons offered by these experiences into the present, we are generally assured a positive future free of obstacles and limitation. The Three Card Spread is essentially a Stepping Stone to Power – one that affords potential healing and clarification on all levels.

Card one: represents your past and the opportunities your experiences are offering you to grow and prosper. The animal depicted on this card clarifies the lessons from the past you would be wise to acknowledge and integrate into your present by answering the why, how and what type questions haunting your mind, thus turning latent negative past experiences into enlightening Gifts of Power.

Card two: represents your present and the beauty that surrounds you at this time. This animal helps you realise the abundance already present in your life by highlighting talents, loves and other gifts from Spirit currently enhancing your life. It anchors the lessons gleaned from the past (card one) so that you may fully integrate the acumen obtained into your life today.

Card three: represents a prospective abundant future and the energies best suited to help you realise it. The animal illustrated on this card is imbued with the wisdom and strength needed to help you break through familiar (and limiting) behaviour and attitudes, to see them for what they are (based on the lessons recognised with cards one and two) and to abandon them in favour of a more productive, more personally relevant set of values and beliefs.

THE BIG FIVE SPREAD

Each continent has its own set of Big Five 'Teacher Creatures'; animals that are viewed with great admiration and respect from a traditional belief-based perspective. Depending on the culture, these animals may have been seen as being the strongest, fastest, most cunning or brave, the cleverest or most blessed by Creation. In some cultures they may have been seen as Ancestor Spirits, offering lessons intended to nurture, teach and protect the people.

According to Native North American philosophy, for example, the Big Five animals often include the Eagle, the Wolf (or the Coyote), Bear, Bison and the Mountain Lion (or Puma), while some African tribes hold the Lion, Cape Buffalo, Rhinoceros, Elephant and the Hippopotamus in highest esteem. The Celts may have looked to the Bull, Cow, Horse, Raven and the Boar for wisdom, while the ancient Aztecs most likely revered the Jaguar, Ocelot, Eagle, Scarlet Macaw and the Serpent. Australia's Indigenous people are still reluctant to speak openly about such things. In reality, I am not sure whether or not they even had such a counsel of sacred animals. Whenever I look within myself to find Australia's sacred Big Five, I have difficulty looking past the Snake, Kangaroo, Emu, Crocodile and Koala.

Personal perception can also be interpreted as projection, so to discover what you perceive as your personal Big Five Animals offers deeper appreciation as to what image you could be projecting. How you view yourself actually reflects how you see the world. Identifying your personal Big Five Animals therefore, is a potent way of projecting a more positive view of yourself. With each animal comes a spiritual lesson that may lift you out of the everyday, the mundane and the emotional confines that currently limit your growth.

Card one depicts the animal best suited to help with the development of lucidity, foresight, intuition and courage. This animal looks at the present. It restores the gift of looking to tomorrow with anticipation. The card in this position offers trust in your inherent knowing without the need for external confirmation. This animal offers excitement, the chance to start again and to see today as the first day of your life. The animal depicted on this card banishes fear, confusion, darkness and despair. It heralds a time of courage, strength of mind, clarity and trust in your intuition.

Card two depicts the animal most competent at reinstating passion into life, as well as innocence, total trust and the ability to take calculated risks when necessary. This animal returns us to that moment when we first experienced true wisdom, clarity and passion; the time when we believed we knew everything and viewed the world from a place of complete trust and expectation. When we looked at the world as a teenager, we did so with complete naivety and innocence. It was when we declared with confidence that 'when I grow up I want to be…' We knew this path offered abundance, strength and everything else that we felt we deserved. It is not what we wanted to be that offers the wisdom, but rather the passion and innocence that inspired us. This card offers the key that may help reclaim that passion and innocence, so that this sacred time of power can be revisited.

Card three depicts the animal most skilled in the gifts of introspection, spiritual journey work, meditation and trust in our inner knowing. This animal invites us to journey within, guiding us to a place of self-trust, self-reliance and self-acceptance. This animal is the one animal that truly illustrates how to best explore our self-perception by reflecting back what others see in us. The animal we find in this position may not be what we are expecting to see, but it will offer insight into the strengths, gifts and potential others see us as having and may suggest areas that need attention, healing or acknowledgment, providing an opportunity for personal growth. You may be shocked, disappointed or thrilled when this card is revealed. Whatever your response, this card offers insight into the unlocking of the whole person Spirit intended you to be.

Card four depicts the animal most learned in the areas of abundance, power, knowledge and wisdom. This animal offers strength in understanding. The card in this position demonstrates the lessons that we have successfully mastered or those that we might want to explore deeper to complete our understanding of who we are and what we are to become. This animal highlights our strengths, our power, the knowledge we have accumulated over a lifetime of learning and the wisdom that we can offer the people. Abundance rarely suggests monetary wealth. It generally reflects those things in our life that we hold the most sacred, and once these facets are identified monetary gain becomes secondary and usually easier to obtain. This animal, therefore, suggests where your true abundance lies, what your power may include and where and when the knowledge you have to offer was first realised within you.

Card five depicts the animal most experienced in the responsibilities that come with leadership, maturity, decision-making and understanding. In tribal communities, the people looked to their leader for direction and inspiration. The leader's responsibilities included making decisions that affected the lives of the people. The leader had to trust their own judgement explicitly without seeking confirmation or approval from the others. With winter approaching the leader would have to know when to pack up camp and where to go and would be expected to provide a stable food source and clean drinking water on arrival, as well as land suitable to support a large dependency of people. The sick, aged and the injured would be left behind to perish if taking them along would impede the tribe's progress; a decision difficult enough to make as the leader, but heartbreaking if the individuals in question were his own child or mother. For the leader to favour an individual member and jeopardise the rest of the clan would have shown them up as being weak and ultimately dangerous. The animal depicted in this position demonstrates how you may best adopt the medicine of the leader. It can show you how you can develop the skills needed to lead your People to a place of greatness; how you can inspire others to strive for greatness, deepen their connection to the Ancestors and heal their past and their families. This animal will help you take responsibility for your own life, your role in the world and your duty as a teacher and wise one. It offers maturity and wisdom and a medicine that comes from a very deep place.

THE WORLD ANIMAL DREAMING TOTEM SPREAD

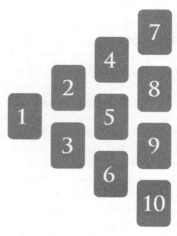

Totem animals can be wild or domestic, native to our country or introduced. Some people refer to introduced animals that have 'gone wild' as 'feral'. We cannot choose our totem animal. This is because our totem animals choose us. Just as you would never rush at an animal in the wild, it is important to treat your totem animals with the same level of respect. Whether an animal is physical in form or etheric in nature, they all react the same way. When an animal feels threatened, for example, it will react in a self-preserving way, but when they're approached with respect, they're more likely to want to interact and become part of our world. Honour your totem animal's energy by representing it in and around your home with statues and ornaments, framed prints, jewellery and so on. By making the animal an obvious part of your physical life, you'll subtly welcome it to become a familiar aspect of your spiritual life as well. You can, and will, attract more than one totem animal. You may feel them with you individually or you may feel totally surrounded by them at times. They will intuitively come into your life when you need them most, and then they will fade away and be 'replaced' by a different energy when the time is right. I have 13 animals that I work with at any one time, and countless others that have come and gone over the years. Totem animals are not the same as power animals. They come and go and are more like 'spiritual friends and helpers' than anything else. And you can have more than one of them. Power animals, though, are permanent. And we only have one. Our power animal echoes our strengths and weaknesses, our wants and desires. If we were able to externalise our soul and have it walk beside us, or if we could transform into an animal and stay in that form forever and never feel like we've been 'ripped off', the animal that emerged would most likely be our power animal. Just like hair and eye colour, facial features and personality traits, totem animals can be 'passed down' from one generation to the next. It is not uncommon, for example, for kids to share the same or similar totems to those of their parents or siblings.

Card one represents the essence of you; the part of you that you hold most sacred. It represents your true inner self and it is where you store your hopes and fears, your plans, secrets and fantasies. This animal can help you better understand this aspect of yourself by offering suggestions as to how you can take advantage of your inherent strengths and potentials. This card may offer personal contests and powerful spiritual investigations that will help you to step out of the shadows.

Card two represents your innate yin (feminine) aspect and **card three** represents your yang (masculine). With the meeting of two opposites that are equal – the light and the dark, the masculine and the feminine, some believe that Creation was born and it was here that life itself began. Every living thing in nature represents Creation. Surrounding all that is Creation is found the Great Mystery, or the essence of all that is known to be unknowable – the core mysteries of life, death and rebirth. Life is about the equal balance of the masculine and the feminine, and only when there is an imbalance does it cause trouble and strife. Masculine energy is typically metaphysical in nature – sunshine, lightning, passion, sexual energy. Feminine energy is very physical in nature and can be touched, seen and felt – the womb, the Earth herself, the bearing of children, the growing of the crops and the nurturing of people. Cards two and three are the balancing forces that support you as a whole person.

Card four governs your personal connection to Spirit and your best line of communication with Great Mystery. If you were to have a direct link to the Creator, then this animal would most likely be it. Embodying how you connect, the reasons for your need to connect and how the Creator may respond, this animal can be called upon to protect you as you sleep, meditate and commune with Spirit.

Card five governs your Earth Walk, the path that you choose to walk as a physical person. This animal demonstrates how you interact with others and how they perceive you. It represents the work you do and the way in which you do it. It can even determine the direction you may want to consider to lift you out of the mundane into a place of spiritual enlightenment and purpose. If the animal turns out to be an animal that frightens you, this animal is trying to initiate change, healing and communication within you. Animals that we are frightened of are our 'shadow totems'. They represent those aspects of ourselves that we are not ready to look at or not prepared to acknowledge. Our shadow totems often symbolise areas where our greatest power lies because they personify our fears, weaknesses and vulnerabilities. If we were to confront these negative attributes and master the lessons they hold, we would emerge stronger, wiser and whole, due largely to the fact that we would no longer be walking in a place of fear.

Card six represents our inner landscape, which is represented by our life experience. It becomes a storeroom for all our memories, subconscious blockages and emotional burdens. It is where we banish the aspects that threaten to weigh us down or allow us to go through life under a veil of fantasy. Our inner landscape affords us greater understanding of the forgotten origins of our pains, fears and insecurities. Just as the Rainbow Serpent shaped the landscape of Mother Earth at the beginning of time, the animal depicted on this card can assist us in the exploration and reshaping (healing) of our inner landscape.

Card seven represents the animal that heralded your birth and was your childhood guardian. It was present at the moment you took your first breath, and was responsible for shaping your personality, your strengths and your gifts of power. It helped you to subconsciously decide what direction your life would take and supported the agreements you made with your spirit family before entering this physical plane. The animal depicted on this card can be called upon to assist in the birth of any new venture, support any movement forward or initiate any new beginnings. Any time that change becomes a necessity, this animal will be there to support the process.

Card eight represents the animal that walked with you during your teenage years. This animal inspired you to strive, achieve and to dare. It offered you great courage, sexual awareness and opened your eyes to potential. It drove you to look into the future and to decide what path your life would follow and channelled the sexual energy that was brewing within you. It is through the eyes of this animal that you declared your life's ambitions.

It is not until we are much older that we wonder where the clarity of the teenage years went. This animal helps us to reclaim this moment of power. It helps us to revisit that energy and drive, that innocence and passion that enabled us to look to the future with wonder, excitement and expectation. This animal supports the energy of the animal in position seven by grounding the innocence and offering a foundation for any new venture or project. By reclaiming the sacred power, we essentially indicate to Spirit that we want another chance to walk our talk and become the person we promised the world we would be.

Card nine represents the animal that supports the transition from the young adult to the parent. The animal depicted on this card offers strength to those who are questioning the value of their life. This animal is the guardian to the inner self. It acts as a mentor, a guide, a beacon of hope and, if allowed, can show you how to master the art of contemplation. This animal will protect you as you meditate and dream. The animal in position nine is the lord of introspection, skilled in the mysteries of journey work and soul retrieval. This animal will take you to a place of deep understanding, inner knowledge and peace. The animal depicted on this card will help you stand in the now, embrace the unknown and trust that all is as it should be. It will teach you to have faith, to find the sacred silence and to not force your destiny by trying to rush it along, or manipulate it into that which it was never meant to be.

Card 10 represents the animal that allows us to look in the mirror and to be pleased with what we see looking back at us. This animal represents you as the elder, wise one and teacher. This animal reminds you when to speak and when to observe. Card 10 indicates our level of maturity, our innate wisdom and the strength that comes with experience. It best highlights your acumen, and the knowledge that will be sought as confirmation by those endeavouring to follow their own path of Spirit. The animal in this position speaks of your integrity, your fidelity and your level of impeccability. This animal is the most sacred. This animal will guide you back to Spirit at the end of your Earth Walk and will be there to witness the weighing of your heart against the Feather of Truth.

THE ANCESTOR SPREAD

We all yearn to take control of our lives and to make a difference to the world. We all have a need to believe in ourselves and to realise our true potential. The realisation that the Earth Mother can nurture within us the wisdom to make these things possible opens a pathway to power for those who seek her counsel. She encourages us to interact on a more productive and fruitful level with our friends and family. She cradles us as we acknowledge our vulnerabilities, face our fears and strive to achieve our dreams.

The **Earth Mother** wants us to remember our Spirit; that we are not apart from the world in which we live, but rather a thread in the universal tapestry; a unique and vital strand in the Web of Life. If left out or ignored the integrity of the universal tapestry would be threatened, thus weakening the potential of the Web of Life. The Earth, therefore, is our Mother.

Grandmother Moon is the protector and nurturer of humanity and just one representation of the Earth Mother's mother. She holds all the mysteries of Creation and, when represented by the Goddess in her many forms, represents all that is feminine.

Her father, **Grandfather Sun**, is a symbol of life, power, action and all that is masculine. Some say that it was birthed by the Raven. Others say that the Sunbird brought the light of the Sun to the world as a symbol of healing energy and a representation of the life-giving seed sent to Mother Earth at the beginning of time, to nurture her children and to impregnate the world with possibility.

Card one the Mother Card, represents your connection to the Earth Mother. It reminds us to honour every living thing as our brother or sister. The stones, the trees, the flowers and the mountains, the animals, birds, insects and fish are all imbued with Spirit. They are all living entities. What may seem inanimate to us is an ambassador of nature and therefore a creature of Spirit. Everything of nature has a lesson to share and wisdom to impart. Card one offers insight into how to access this knowledge, how to deepen your connection with the Earth, and how to best honour Spirit's ways.

Card two The Grandmother Card, highlights the need to honour the primary feminine influences in your life – the mothers, grandmothers, sisters, wives and daughters. This card asks you to look at the interaction you hold with the women in your life and to look to the animal depicted to help deepen, heal or initiate a more meaningful relationship with one or all of them. If a relationship with one of the women in your life has ended for whatever reason, the animal portrayed on this card may offer support, understanding or counsel as to the reasons, lessons and the potential hidden behind the experience.

Card three the Grandfather Card, highlights the need to honour the primary masculine influences in your life – the fathers, grandfathers, the brothers, husbands and sons. This card asks you to look at the interaction you hold with the men in your life and to look to the animal depicted to help deepen, heal or initiate a more meaningful relationship with one or all of them. If a relationship with one of the men in your life as ended for whatever reason, the animal portrayed on this card may offer support, understanding or counsel as to the reasons, lessons and the potential hidden behind the experience.

CARD INTERPRETATIONS
THE ANIMALS AND THEIR SACRED MESSAGES

He [Great Spirit] only sketches out the path of life roughly for all the creatures on earth, shows them where to go, where to arrive, but leaves them to find their own way to get there. He wants them to act independently according to their nature, to the urges of each of them.
Lame Deer, LAKOTA

EAST / AIR
GOLDEN YELLOW

BALD EAGLE
ONENESS

I grew up believing myself to be forsaken, alone and isolated. When a car accident took the lives of two boys I knew as brothers, I felt as though the Universe itself had conspired against me and my life spiralled into a vortex of confusion and despair. Refusing to be broken, the accident reignited the spiritual fire that had nurtured me since the day I was born; a fire that continues to warm and inspire me to this day. By losing the brothers, I miraculously found myself. While my familiar self also died that night, my true self was reborn. I realised I wasn't alone anymore. In receiving the lesson of loss I simultaneously gained the gift of oneness. While the boys had gone from this world, they had returned to the Creator Spirit to be reunited with the source of all life. Their essence was all around me. I felt an alliance with the world and sensed that I was surrounded by Spirit.

If the Bald Eagle has soared into your cards today, you are being reminded that God doesn't just live 'out there' and that being close to God doesn't need to be difficult. The day I realised I had fooled myself into believing that God didn't care about me was the day I personally found Spirit. I realised that God did care, but I felt it easier to believe when I referred to 'God' as 'Spirit'. Bald Eagle (as an emissary of the Creator Spirit) suggests that perhaps, like me, you have been using the 'wrong' words and looking to God from the 'wrong' perspective and suggests you try using the word 'Spirit'. You may feel a stronger connection to that word and with Spirit as your ally, you will feel confident to march out into the world and find yourself. You will feel that you are one of the people, not apart from them. Spirit is our link to Creation. Spirit inspired Creation. Spirit is Creation. It refers to those in Spirit and it is the life force found within all things. It is God but it is also the Goddess. It's the Angels, your spirit guides, your totems and the Faeries. It is the life-force found in water, fire, wind and earth. It is the power of thought, the emotion of love, the power of silence and the process known as death. It is you. And it is the people. Spirit binds us together and makes us 'One'. And the Bald Eagle card is reminding you that you are 'One'; 'One *with* The One'.

ANTELOPE
RADIANCE

The Antelope is sacred to Astarte, the Middle Eastern Goddess of balance, holding death and destruction in one hand and birth and regeneration in the other. Known as Hathor in Ancient Egypt and Demeter in Ancient Greece, her name means 'Queen of the Stars'. Astarte watches over the souls of the departed, cladding them lovingly in robes of light and calling them her 'star children'. Astarte's horns resemble those of the Antelope. Like Astarte, the Antelope is a guide: a source of light that showers optimism and inspiration down upon the people. In fact, it could be said that Astarte is the spirit of the Morning Star that holds the light during an otherwise dark and confusing night.

If the Antelope has pronked her way into your cards today, you are being reminded that no matter what happens in your life, Spirit will always provide a guiding light, a symbol of hope and a way of leading you out of the darkness. This darkness is very much like night-time. All things seem difficult and more overwhelming when the world is dark and everyone is asleep, and that's because there's nothing you can do to bring closure to a situation or heal the issues surrounding it. Your hands are tied. You are forced to sit and wait; wait for the sun to rise, for clarity to return and for an opportunity to present that allows you to do something about it. And when the Morning Star shines through your window, banishing the darkness and lighting up your room, Antelope asks that you see the light as a sign of affirmation that heralds radiant new beginnings and the dawn of a new day. In order for anything to be born, any project to start or any new relationship to begin, though, some aspect of your life must be allowed to die. Old doors must shut before new ones open. And it is the Antelope who steps up to the mark and helps channel the process, with the simple promise that everything will work out for the best.

LION
LANGUOR

Every morning, the Lion holds his head up and shakes his golden mane as if heralding the dawn of a new day. He is powerfully confident, hardworking, inspirational and creative. If he has a cause that inspires him or offers him purpose, Lion has the ability to do anything and manifest whatever he puts his mind to. In fact, whatever he touches turns to gold. It's like he has the 'Midas Touch'. While he is a powerful and majestic creature when he is in his power though, the shadow side of Lion asks that his mate do all the domestic work: the hunting, defending and raising the young. Sadly, such an expectation is a trait indicative of many men today. As if echoing the attitude of the modern male, Lion bravely invites us to ponder the wellbeing of our relationships and how we perceive ourselves and others.

If the Lion has proudly marched his way into your cards today, you are being reminded that you are both highly intelligent and capable of bringing all your visions to fruition. You are being promised warmth, protection and compelling opportunity to shine, as long as you avoid laziness and the tendency to feel unmotivated that often plagues you. If you're looking for encouragement, a gentle boost to your ego or even confirmation that you're on the right track, then see the appearance of the Lion card the sign you've been looking for. It comes suggesting that you're soon to realise your potential. Lion promises great things, but needs constant confirmation and proof of his power and the important role he plays in the world. He offers abundance and power, realisation, clarity and inner strength, particularly after a time of confusion, darkness and dormancy; like the new dawn that comes after a long, dark night. Lion says, 'Stop procrastinating and get on with it'. Languor is a limiting behaviour often rooted in fear. Motivation is a decision. Self-confidence is a birth-rite. Remember this, and you can (and will) achieve great things.

RHINOCEROS
STAYING POWER

The mysterious Unicorn ('uni' meaning one, and 'corn' meaning horn) is a medieval symbol of virtue, entitlement and splendour. According to legend, only the purest of heart and body could approach, tame and harness the Unicorn, usually a young virginal maiden. When tales of a magickal single-horned beast reached the people, any creature that had a single horn protruding from its forehead was immediately assumed to be the Unicorn. The Rhinoceros' horn was then targeted as a source of supernatural and therapeutic power; a fascination that, unfortunately, still lingers to this day. It was once erroneously believed to cure ailments such as impotence, worms, epilepsy, vertigo, fever, stomach ache, convulsions and smallpox.

If the Rhinoceros has charged his way into your cards today, you are energetically being offered a form of staying power and a way to process any source of dis-ease. While the horn of the Rhino offers no restorative properties on the physical level, it does offer the power and might to help you spiritually push through anything that threatens your sense of wellbeing. The spiritually sensitive, antenna-like horn of the Unicorn Rhinoceros detects poisonous thoughts and intentions, negative vibrations and dark-side entities (a belief that still holds true in the Middle and Far East), deflecting them with ease. It also clears obstacles and unwanted interferences, while banishing fear, illness and grief from your consciousness. Phallic in form, the horn quickly manifests new beginnings in their place, encouraging fertility and advancement. Whenever you require help moving forward or upward in life, visualise the Rhinoceros walking ahead of you with its powerful horn lowered, pushing forward, clearing restrictions and limiting beliefs and behaviour out of the way. Offering determination and staying power, the Rhinoceros will ensure a fertile, productive life full of the things you innately know you deserve, despite what others may say or think to the contrary.

CHEETAH
VIGOUR

Cheetahs are built for speed. Practically every part of the Cheetah is adapted to maximise its potential. Despite the incredible speeds the Cheetah can reach (up to 114 kilometres per hour), it is very demanding on them physically and they can only maintain such a pace for about 275 metres before needing to rest deeply.

If the Cheetah has raced into your cards today, you may be fretting too much about body image, health and fitness ... or rather, what others think of you on a superficial level. You may be trying to do too much; trying too hard to gain approval, acknowledgment or prove a point. It's all about personal pacing and self-acceptance with Cheetah. She knows how much she can do and doesn't bully herself to do any more than she can achieve. She's comfortable in her own skin. She doesn't waste her time or energy worrying about being lazier, fatter, weaker or older than those around her. It's true that she's always racing about and rarely has a day off, but she's able to manage her hectic lifestyle because she knows how to pace herself. Only when she's not listening to her inner voice and her body does she worry that she's unsupportive or self-indulgent and may even suffer from skin allergies, high blood pressure and stress. So, if Cheetah has visited you today, you're probably feeling a tad overwhelmed, emotional and unable to hide how you feel. It may seem that issues from the past, unresolved hurts or grief have come back to haunt you and that all you want to do is curl up and hide. Cheetah encourages you to do just the opposite, though. Instead of going it alone, Cheetah suggests you spend some quality time with members of your own sex; your friends, family and associates from work. In doing so, you will find yourself rebuilding stamina, morale and personal authentication. You will find yourself feeling more relaxed because you've given your mind a chance to slow down. By listening to Cheetah, you will find yourself returning to a state of true health and wellbeing, deepening your relationships and your own integrity on a level more personal than you've ever achieved previously.

PHEASANT
LOVERS

Revered as a symbol of light in China, the Pheasant is celebrated as the epitome of honesty and wealth, a creature believed to bring luck and success. In Japan, the Pheasant brings thunder, suggesting a powerful ability to control and focus passion, to channel energy productively and to willingly embrace necessary change. The Pheasant is a bird that knows commitment and heart-felt devotion. They understand the tender, unconditional and protective love a mother feels for her child, for example, and the genuine affection you may feel for a dear friend. Offering strength and endurance to those determined to better themselves through study and scholarly achievement, the Pheasant educates us in the art of self-love so that we may appreciate ourselves and our abilities more and, being a bird that mates for life, bonding with one particular mate, the Pheasant also teaches us to trust, to open our hearts and to commit deeply to romantic relationships, both old and new.

If Pheasant has graced your cards today, you're being primed for a positive and harmonious connection with another person or other people, or the deepening of a relationship already well established. Supporting any form of bonding, from a new lover, an engagement or marriage, through to a new boss or workplace, new friends, a new doctor, specialist, teacher, Pheasant is also well-equipped to take you deep within yourself to where your yin aspect may be uniting with your yang for the very first time; where your feminine may be melding with your masculine, the two opposites that are equal coming together to help you develop a broader perception of the world, a deeper spiritual awareness, a more passionate and determined ability to create your heart's desire or the knowledge of how to formulate and birth your dreams into reality. If it's not a relationship with another person that the Pheasant is suggesting, then it's perhaps the realisation of a new and healthy relationship developing between you and yourself; one that will lead to the manifestation of things previously only talked about.

HORNED OWL
WARNING

Horned Owls get their name from the pair of large 'ear tufts' with which they communicate. When aggravated, the tufts lay flat against their head, when they're curious, the tufts stand erect. For many, the Owl evokes a sense of mystery as a silent flyer and a creature of the night, the embodiment of death, magick, deception and negative influence, not to be trusted. On the other hand, it is also revered as a powerful teacher and ally; a guide that navigates us through life with some degree of clarity, intuitive knowing and wisdom. Equally, the Owl is a powerful symbol of prophecy, secrets and higher knowledge.

If the Horned Owl has swooped silently into your cards today, BE WARNED! According to superstitious belief, seeing a Horned Owl in the wild comes as a forewarning of menace and misfortune. Houses and other buildings inhabited by Horned Owls are generally presumed haunted because they are known to comfortably handle the unsettling energies of restless spirits and 'ghosts'. These warnings are based on superstition and fear and not on the Owl's true wisdom. There is no animal in creation that brings bad luck or ill fortune to anyone 'unlucky' enough to see it in the wild. Ask the Horned Owl, 'What are you trying to tell me; do you have a message of warning for me?' Perhaps you have something that's 'haunting' your mind or heart, or causing you concern. Perhaps something from the past has resurfaced, bringing with it 'ghosts' that threaten to raise issues long believed to be 'dead and buried'. Perhaps a troublesome person you once considered a friend has reappeared in your life or a change in fortune has caused you some concern. Horned Owl lends its eyes so that you may see in the dark by revealing lies or dishonesty that threaten to limit your growth, dampen your potential and cause doubt regarding your personal judgment. It sits up all night and waits for the sun to rise and, as such, is a bird of illumination and clarity. To have the Horned Owl visit your cards is a warning that things you assume are sound may not be as reliable as you had hoped or assumed. It reveals things trying to remain hidden, camouflaged and undetectable to trusting eyes.

BUTTERFLY TRANSFORMATION

Butterflies are insects capable of flight thanks to two pairs of large, scaly wings. But before they looked like this, all Butterflies began life as a Caterpillar. When they have grown big enough, Caterpillars ready themselves for their final moult that will see them pupate, or become a chrysalis. Although it appears from the outside that nothing much is happening, inside the chrysalis an incredible amount of activity is taking place. The Caterpillar is literally changing in every way. In truth, its anatomy is being chemically pulled apart and put back together into the form we know to be the Butterfly! The process is quite traumatic (some might even say 'painful') for the Caterpillar; wings suddenly sprout from where none were before, prolegs and crochets disappear and a pair of antennae emerges from their forehead. It's an exhausting progression that takes up to two weeks to complete.

If the Butterfly has fluttered by your cards today, you're being prepared for a magickal transformation, a chance to make sense of what may have been a traumatic and potentially 'painful' period of necessary change. Butterfly offers new life and the chance to transform on all levels, to become a stronger, prouder person who's more willing to trust. As the Butterfly moves from Caterpillar to Butterfly, it shows trust in its ability to grow and adapt. The Caterpillar is slow and cumbersome, symbolic of how we view ourselves as we struggle to come to terms with new information and to adapt to what this new information demands of us. And then we find ourselves going within, contemplating and sifting through all that we have learned. As the Caterpillar becomes the chrysalis and readies to metamorphose, we begin to internalise our newfound wisdom. We examine and question, file and discard. By the time the Caterpillar decides to emerge as the Butterfly, we're also ready to present our newfound wings and our need to share our wisdom and, from a place of experience, enhance the lives of others. The sight of the Butterfly breaking free of its chrysalis is a re-enactment of rebirth. As such, the Butterfly is a powerful symbol for anyone contemplating change or who is in the midst of major transformation.

HORSE
PERSONAL POWER

When Horses first made their way into our world, they offered us the gift of physical freedom like nothing had ever done before. They offered their backs to human riders, allowed themselves to be harnessed to carriages, chariots, barges and boats, stagecoaches, wagons, trams and ploughs and were used to pull milling stones, to support windmills and waterwheels. As a result, Horse understands the true meaning of Personal Power – that inherent knowing or wisdom that resides deep within our soul as a spiritual gift or a personal philosophy based on life experience or a sense of greater purpose that ensures we never give up without a fight; an invisible force that drives us onward and upward, constantly whispering in our ear a promise to reveal the purpose of our existence here on Earth.

If Horse has pranced its way into your cards today, you're being reminded of what it means to be unique and sacred and to channel that knowledge into remembering your Personal Power. You realised it the moment you were conceived, and you made a promise at that point to never forget it, to embrace it as you grew and to teach others how to reclaim theirs should they ever forget, that your Personal Power would never be wasted or held so tight that it suffocated. Personal Power is knowledge and wisdom accumulated over lifetimes of experience. When knowledge is gathered and used for the betterment of the self and others, it gathers in energy which builds in momentum, becoming passion that offers motivation to move forward, to grow and to expand on all levels. Personal Power is awareness that comes from being connected to Spirit and all things of Nature. It offers the opportunity to enhance the world and to make life richer for others, and it is what future generations will remember you for when you finally return to Spirit. If Horse has appeared in your cards today, put your ears back and gallop in the first direction that takes your fancy. Travel to every corner of the spiritual globe because by journeying 'out' into the world, you will get to know your inner-self on a much deeper level. Don't be timid and don't give up before you start. Just take a step forward. It doesn't matter what direction you take initially in your quest to realise Personal Power because, so long as you take that first step to uncovering it, you will find it eventually.

OTTER
PLAYFULNESS

Every time I visit my local zoo, I always head straight for the Otters. I love the way they look up at me, chattering, looking this way and that as if to say 'Come on! Jump in! No one's looking! Come and have a swim with me! Is that food? Go on, throw me some. No one's looking!' There might be a small crowd gathered to watch them as they go about making their mischief, but they're oblivious of the people, focused solely on inspiring a sense of fun and spontaneity. Otter is a creature of light-hearted charm; a mischievous feminine being that harnesses the energy of water and earth. She helps us balance the joy found in being spontaneous and playful with the practicalities and responsibilities of living a routine life. She encourages us to 'loosen up' and to be less serious and anxious.

If Otter has charmed its way into your cards today, you're being asked to express your emotions and to be more open with your feelings. You're being offered the chance to return to a state of child-like innocence. She appears in our cards when we need to be nurtured and encouraged to play and be impulsive and joyful. So, take her advice because Otter is asking you to take pleasure in the little things, to take time out for yourself and to indulge in some fun and adventure. Take up a hobby for example, or enrol in a class or take yourself off on a holiday. Despite encouraging us to be playful and spontaneous though, Otter isn't frivolous. She knows and understands responsibility, and is not one to shun them in favour of having a good time. Instead, she helps us find pleasure in the more mundane aspects of life: the chores and jobs that may weigh us down, frustrate us or cause us to resent others. Otter shifts our perception so that we may see them as essential and blessed aspects of life, duties that may not be there if not for the treasured people, gifts and opportunities that make up our world.

GHOST BAT
REBIRTH

It's an ancient European belief that when someone dies in their sleep, the soul takes the form of a Bat in its bid to fly back to the Creator Spirit. This was mainly because the Bat, the only mammal capable of true flight, is typically seen at night. Some of Australia's Indigenous people share the sacred view that the Bat offers regeneration, embodying the souls of men who have passed, while some Native Americans believe the Bat personifies the 'Shaman's Death'; a sacred rebirth rite that sees the initiate emerge from the ritualistic cave a fully trained shaman. The initiate often experiences a form of ritualistic death before their training begins, where the familiar world they know literally falls apart due to extreme loss, grief, illness or some other personal catastrophe and finds himself or herself stripped of all sense of 'normality', their view of the world broken down to the most basic of levels. Before the initiate breaks down, a trigger activates his or her decline, a decline that is usually 'signed' by Spirit as a powerful dream experienced by a prominent member or Elder who sees it as a significant occurrence worthy of deeper exploration. The initiate is then tested, trained and 'qualified', whereby they are totally pulled apart mentally and spiritually and 'rebuilt' on all levels to emerge as an individual who walks as one with the spirit world.

To have the Bat fly into your cards comes as a sign that you're about to go through a period of ritualistic rebirth, but not before experiencing necessary change, closure or symbolic 'death'. Just as a baby rests inverted in the womb waiting for its birth, the Bat hangs upturned in its cave waiting for night to fall. The cave has long been seen symbolically as the womb of the Earth Mother. Wrapped in its wings, the Bat waits for the right moment to release its grip and exit as if rebirthing itself into the physical world. The appearance of the Bat denotes a desire for a new beginning or the chance to start from scratch; to completely rebirth who and what you are, as if re-emerging from your mother's womb as a brand-new being. Bat heralds a symbolic death, a sudden ending or closure, followed by an obvious new beginning offering the chance for expansion and growth. It supports us as we abandon old patterns and let go of fear and prepares us for rebirth, symbolised by the stepping into a new phase or chapter of life.

POLAR BEAR BROTHERHOOD

Polar Bears are also known as Yellow Bears, White Bears and Northern Bears. While the Polar Bear is born white and may turn yellow as it matures, they actually have transparent fur and black skin. When the sun reflects off the transparent fur, it looks white. The people of the North revere the Polar Bear as a source of great spiritual power, physical endurance and wisdom and it is considered as family and their kin, with many believing they are its direct descendants. To some, the Polar Bear is an ancestor, a brother considered superior to man. To others, it is an incarnated spirit, or the physical embodiment of a soul that has passed over. Legend tells of men shape-shifting into Polar Bears and vice versa.

The Polar Bear is the 'Spirit of the North', an animal of ancient knowledge and wisdom that guards the Gates to the Spirit World. It is a teacher, guide and mentor of great authority.

If the Polar Bear has lumbered its way into your cards today, you're being offered a deep and meaningful insight into the world of Spirit. You're about to go on a hands-on journey into the other realms, to experience the joys that are to be found there. Whether through your dreams, visions had during meditation or via some other means, the Polar Bear is promising to open the portal that bridges our world with the Dreamtime. The Dreamtime was the time before time that witnessed the Creation of the world, when animals could become man and man could become animal. It will bring you back, too, to your own personal point of Creation, when you first realised that the power to dream, decide and formulate your future was yours. Polar Bear is offering you the chance to re-assess your beliefs, your values and your personal commitment to walk gently upon the Earth by helping you to feel good and proud to live in your own skin once again. With Polar Bear watching over you, you will be part of the world, not apart from it. Polar Bear ignites the desire to begin a spiritual quest that will see your life regain its integrity, wholesomeness and clarity; where your gifts of power emerge, your purpose realised and your connection to Spirit become comfortable, deeper and inherently abundant.

NORTH / FIRE
OCHRE RED

MEERKAT
DEPENDABILITY

Meerkats are highly social creatures. Each member of the family is allocated a specific role or responsibility. Climbing to the highest point they can find, one acts as sentry, keeping a keen eye out for danger. A babysitter cares for the young, while others hunt and gather food. Meerkats hold the wellbeing of others as their first priority, knowing that in doing so they benefit themselves. I don't think there's a person alive that doesn't have a sense of ambition on some level. Many of us would love to follow a path that nourishes them and their family, and what better way to achieve such a dream than striving to better yourself inside and out while being a dependable, reliable source of support for others?

If Meerkat has scampered headlong into your cards today, you're being reminded that when you allow yourself to be of service to others, especially selflessly and without expectation, your efforts will be invariably noticed in and rewarded or repaid in kind. The reward may come in the form of a healthy pay rise or bonus, verbal praise or some other form of recognition. When you selflessly help others in the reaching of their goals by offering time or labour, you open yourself up to the favour being returned by them. When Meerkat creeps into your cards, you know it's time to offer support, assistance and generosity because when you do you're actually creating space for the same to be offered to you someday. When you yearn to achieve a goal, but you cannot achieve it alone, to put your personal plans into 'go slow' in favour of helping someone else realise theirs will often see your dreams come to fruition sooner than expected. Meerkat understands that when you work as a team, helping the most agile climber among you to reach the top of the termite mound, everyone benefits. Meerkat believes that it doesn't matter who reaches the top first, so long as someone does. In doing so, everyone gets the chance to step up and view the world from a wider perspective.

WILDEBEEST
THE VICTIM

Wildebeest is a powerful ally. Its survival instinct guides us through periods of confusion, apprehension and hurt until we find the strength to put our foot down and say 'no more'. It provides the skills and strategies we sometimes need to face life's challenges alone while keeping our integrity intact. In its shadow phase, though, the Wildebeest reverts to herd mentality, when the members of a group act together without any planning or direction. For example, when grazing, if one animal moves, the whole herd moves. If one animal is startled and begins to run, the rest of the herd follows as one. During migration, hundreds of animals die each year as they try to cross fast-flowing rivers, desperately trying to reach the opposite bank. Wildebeest warns of such dangers: the risk of being propelled by the need to be loved, peer-group pressure, popular belief, the will of others or even mass hysteria.

If the Wildebeest has blundered its way into your cards today, you're being warned that you could be giving your power over to someone or something else too willingly, which runs the risk of losing your sacred individuality. You become 'just another one of a mob'. You sell yourself short, you lose your voice and you may even act irrationally, aggressively or become blind to perils. Seeking another's help or counsel is positive when you maintain your own sense of truth. Congregating is to come together in a positive way and benefits the group as a whole because it's empowered by individual consent. Being overly trusting or relying too heavily on others for guidance and support, however, often suggests a lack of trust in your own self-worth, inner wisdom and your natural ability to make decisions. It tends to hamper your vision, restrict your movement and limit your choice. When Wildebeest appears in the cards, it comes demanding that you take stock of your life, take responsibility for your actions and begin nurturing yourself. It abhors the victim mindset and the herd mentality because it knows that it only encourages the 'it wasn't my fault' attitude and the limiting belief that you cannot succeed in life unless you're supported, loved or empowered by another.

ZEBRA
INDIVIDUALITY

Zebras are best known for their unique stripe patterns. The mares give birth to a single foal. Immediately after birth, the foal sets about memorising its mother's stripe pattern so that it can identify her from the other females. Also known as the 'Tiger-Horse', Zebra imbues us with courage enough to identify and embrace our Personal Power by helping us recognise just how unique and magickal we are as individuals. No two Zebras share the same stripe pattern. Like the human fingerprint, Zebra stamps on the common notion that to belong, we can't be exclusive; that to be a part of something, we must comply with popular belief and lose our identity; that to feel welcome, we must become a mirror of everyone else; that to be a part of the whole, we must first submit to becoming just another number. This attitude confuses the Zebra who, while acknowledging her sacred bond with the rest of the herd, refuses to conform or give in. Instead, she reminds us that if we yearn to realise what our life purpose is and why we are here, we must first embrace our sacred independence.

If the Zebra has trotted its way into your cards today, you're being reminded that, while we may all look superficially the same at first glance, we each carry a unique genetic blueprint. By combining wisdom of the Tiger and the Horse, Zebra has essentially cantered into your life to help you combat fear and insecurity and acknowledge your personal Gifts of Power. She encourages us to put our ears back and to gallop in the first direction that takes our fancy, to explore the world while engaging fully in the journey and integrating the lessons we experience along the way. Zebra adds that there's no point embarking on the journey if you're planning on following it the same way as everyone else. Instead, add your own flavour to it; make it yours. Stop pretending that you're happy being 'just one of the crowd' and begin seeing yourself as, worthy of being heard. You have something to offer. You can – and will – make a difference because you hold within your heart sacred knowledge that no one else has, and now is the time to remember it, to unveil it and share it with the world.

TIGER
COWARDICE

The Tiger's stripes afford it perfect camouflage in the tall grass and abundant brushwood where it stalks its prey There are ancient stories that tell of mysterious, supernatural Tigers that mimic human behaviour, live in villages and feed on human flesh. However, man-eating Tigers are rare but the rubber harvesters still wear masks on the back of their heads as a precaution, knowing that Tigers generally prefer to take their prey from behind. Tiger, although imbued with incredible physical power and beauty, is a somewhat clumsy hunter. Rumour has it that about 80% of all their strikes go unrewarded because of what could be misconstrued as a 'lack of confidence' or fear. The Tiger's apprehension forces it to lie still, anticipating its quarry's every move and waiting for the perfect opportunity to pounce. Suddenly, it bursts from the undergrowth, leaping onto its prey's back, biting down on its neck, puncturing the jugular. Thus, proving it is no coward but rather a beast that knows exactly what it wants. The trouble is Tiger displays a sense of awkwardness when it comes to confrontation.

If the Tiger has crept silently into your cards today, you're being urged to look at that which you dread the most in the eye and defiantly take it on. Instead of 'beating around the bush' or ignoring the problems that hinder your progress in the vain hope that they will simply go away, Tiger reminds you of your inherent beauty, inner strength and sense of resolve. To have the Tiger appear in your cards is to be encouraged to harness your potential as truth, and see yourself worthy of greatness. Speak openly and from the heart instead of holding in your fears. If you have concerns regarding a friend or family member, confront them with love instead of talking about them behind their back. Or if you think others have concerns about you, then raise the question and be brave enough to hear the answer. Reject the shadow aspect of the Tiger, which may label you as a coward. Instead, be like the Peacock – the Tiger's ideal prey – and seek to integrate the way of the impeccable warrior into your life by vowing to always walk your talk and face your personal demons head on.

ANT
STRENGTH

Ants may be exceptionally small, but they make up for it with incredible strength. While some Ants have mandibles or pincers so large that they seem over-sized in comparison to the rest of their body, enabling them to carry many times their own body weight and to fight off aggressors, Ants also depend on patience, team work and strength of mind to anticipate and outsmart their opponent's every move. A schemer and engineer, Ant demonstrates the ability to move a mountain, one grain of sand at a time. Not only does this take a great deal of physical strength and endurance, but also immense mental resolve, determination and patience. It can be a tad overwhelming to see your kitchen bench covered in what seems like millions of Ants as they take advantage of the open sugar basin, a droplet of honey or spilled fruit juice. When this next happens, realise it's not the Ants you need to take notice of, but instead, the message they have to share.

If Ant has scuttled into your cards today, thank the Ant in advance for its lesson because you're about to receive a personal Master Class in Patience! Patience is the ultimate and noblest form of strength any person can display. As an unknown author once wrote, *'Patience is waiting. Not passively waiting. That is laziness. But to keep going when the going is hard and slow – that is patience.'* So, if Ant has wandered into your life, take it as a sign that perhaps you're greatest strength is NOT patience, and perhaps you're being a little lazy in bringing something to fruition or you're pushing for something to happen long before it is ready. Being lazy could mean that perhaps you're waiting for someone else to realise a dream for you, or that you've invested hope instead of effort into shaping an idea into reality. Alternatively, perhaps you're pushing for something to happen before its time, which often means pushing it further away. I refer to these scenarios as 'away towards'. The more you push toward something that's not ready to be realised often sees it moving further away. Surrendering and accepting that all will be revealed in its own time will see you realise your dreams, especially when you keep going even when the going is hard and slow.

COYOTE
THE JOKER

Coyote is a practical joker and trickster who will willingly break the rules shaped by the gods or Mother Nature herself, oftentimes with an accidental yet positive outcome, by means of trickery or even thievery. Coyote plays tricks and games in a bid to raise awareness and, for this reason, he is considered cunning, foolish, funny and even sacred. Coyote was said to have stolen fire from the gods, for example, and then gave it to the human race. He is typically described as omnipresent, appearing in some stories as the Creator who formed the people from clay and breathed life into them. To others he is a messenger, a fool or a clown, a charming young man or an animal, while for others the Coyote is more of a sacred energy. Coyote is one for learning through laughter and jokes and forces us to laugh at ourselves, see the folly of our ways and learn from our mistakes. By mocking us, Coyote forces us to question our beliefs, testing our commitment to them. He shows them up as being shallow and groundless or reassures us of their integrity by accidentally proving their merit, anchoring them as viable aspects of our world view.

If Coyote has swindled his way into your cards today, he's probably done so to make fun of the earnestness and blind dedication you waste on habits and beliefs that are no longer valid or purposeful to your life. He is well-equipped to initiate heightened levels of awareness by encouraging us to trip over our egos in order to regain humility and balance. Coyote reminds us that enlightenment is best found in experience, with every experience offering learning and a chance to better ourselves. Coyote does not see it as dishonourable to be the recipient of a valuable practical joke, especially when that joke offers sacred learning. Jokes that belittle and tarnish our self-worth are not respectable jokes, however, and are not those practised by Coyote. He combines all things prudent with the imprudent; the revered with the disrespected. It calls for us to laugh and be laughed at. It unites all things opposite. It encourages us to throw caution to the wind, to experience trial and error and to learn from our mistakes. It returns us to a state of child-like innocence and allows us to find the wonder in simple discoveries. It teaches us to experience pleasure, shun fear and apprehension and to celebrate life.

BEE POTENTIAL

Bees are largely communal creatures that build nests occupied by permanent swarms. The drones have special glands in their abdomens that convert sugar into honey which they then eat to become wax. The wax is then used to create the cells in which the larvas are grown and honey is stored. Bees were once revered as bridges between the physical world and the Underworld. Images of Bees decorated the walls of Greek tombs which were sometimes built to resemble bee hives. Bees were revered as the embodiment of the souls of priestesses, known as 'Melissae' (which means 'Bees'), who had dedicated their lives to Aphrodite, the golden honeycomb.

If Bee has swarmed your cards today, you're being encouraged to celebrate life, to acknowledge your potential and to make good of the golden opportunities you're being offered. In my world, 'honey equals money'; liquid gold that drips from the hive like an over-full bag of coins. Having the Bee fly into your cards is like being offered the realisation that anything is possible and that any project, thought or dream can be brought abundantly to fruition with trust, passion and determination. Bee endorses the value of organised community, dedicated team work and the realisation of a dream through group effort and combined vision. In order to reach a desired level of achievement or to build the strongest of foundations in life, it's often a good idea to enlist the support and knowledge of others who are willing to work toward the common good, just as drone Bees demonstrate loyalty and commitment to their Queen. Bee nurtures us as we celebrate the magic of life and discover the wonder and fertility in every experience. Bee may have come to you today to help you conceive a child, for example, or to birth your own business or get a new project off the ground. Bee provides a fertile foundation on which any 'seed' of thought or want may take root, grow and provide abundance. If it's a business you'd like to establish, the key is to see yourself as the Queen Bee. See your vision grow so abundantly that 'Drones' are required, after which you can either sit back and rest or leave them to continue what you started so that you can move on to create yet another 'hive'.

GORILLA ESSENCE

Despite their powerful appearance, Gorillas are gentle vegetarians who prefer to discourage confrontation by beating their chest, baring their large teeth and hooting aggressively. They represent our potential to overcome the greatest of obstacles with a sense of gentleness, unconditional love, trust and commitment. Gorillas eat plants and rarely take the lives of other animals for food. They cry, dream and hold hopes for their children, just as we do. In fact Gorillas share 97% of the same DNA as humans, making them one of our closest living relatives in the animal kingdom. To embrace Gorilla is to return to our essence and to consider the things that make our heart sing. Ask yourself, what do I truly love doing?

What is my passion? Why not turn your passion into an income? A life that offers no personal reward or enjoyment is not a life worth living. Gorilla asks that we be honest, gentle and loyal to ourselves instead of beating our chest in a vain attempt to appear strong and powerful, while running the risk of burning ourselves out mentally and physically because of expectation and tradition.

If Gorilla has wandered into your cards today, you are being primed for a time of personal reflection. Gorilla invites us to consider where we could be gentler, fairer and more honest with ourselves. Being that Gorilla will do everything in its power to avoid confrontation, to have it appear in your cards suggests that you tend to overlook or ignore important issues in your life in favour of keeping peace. Gorilla asks that you take your responsibilities seriously, but not to the extent that you begin to believe the world may collapse in a heap if you shift your attention to taking care of yourself a little. Instead of living your life solely to make others happy; instead of only feeling safe and secure when those around you are at peace, or pretending to be content with your lot in life when you are grieving for change or yearning to follow your heart, Gorilla comes beating his chest in a bid to encourage you to address the things that may offer you freedom and joy and to act upon them today, without bullying others – or yourself – in the process.

GREY WOLF
THE PATHFINDER

Grey Wolves are social animals, living in family groups of between six to 10 individuals. Each pack contains a dominant breeding pair: an 'alpha' male and female, subordinate adults, the dominant breeding pair's current pups and usually the previous year's pups. In order for an animal of lesser standing to attain breeding status, it can either remain with the natal pack, or leave and start its own pack. Remaining with the family group means running the risk of never achieving dominance, while leaving makes them vulnerable to attack While they're probably more than happy to remain with the pack, individuals are sometimes forced to venture out into the world to search (as the Lone Wolf) for new and greater wisdom. Because of this, Grey Wolf is traditionally the totem of the teacher, pioneer and guide.

If Grey Wolf has howled his way into your cards today, you are being encouraged to break away from conventional belief, organised religion, family settings, regular jobs, and any other structured system that limits or shuns creative thinking and free-spirited ideals. Grey Wolf instils a strong sense of self, purpose and direction, and invites you to respectfully put all your conformist thought patterns and time-honoured values aside to develop a whole new set that nurtures you. It's pushing you to leave your comfort zone, explore new ground and establish new and personal values and beliefs. Those drawn to the Grey Wolf usually find themselves breaking away from structure and order to explore the broader, subtler realms of life. They become 'students', seeking out credible teachers, mentors and elders with the intention of learning, discovering and remembering why they're here and what they're supposed to do. If this is you, trust that you will absorb all that is relevant. It may feel daunting now, but the day will soon arrive that will see you 'graduate' or feel compelled to end your quest for knowledge and return home. Armed with newfound wisdom and sacred knowledge, you will share what you have learned, thus enhancing the spiritual foundation of your clan.

SKUNK
COMPROMISE

Typically coloured black and white, Skunks are renowned for their foul-smelling spray, which they eject as a defence from the base of their tail. The odour is so terrible that it deflects the attention of even the most formidable predators. Skunk is fascinated by human nature. She loves to study human character, attitudes and how we view ourselves. She finds it intriguing how our innate sense of self-worth fluctuates, serving us well one day and almost punishing us the next, ultimately affecting our self-perception and how others view us. Skunk is an easygoing soul; private, quiet, casual, living an uncluttered and balanced life. Her black-and-white fur coat demonstrates true harmony between her yin and yang (feminine and masculine), as well as a healthy honouring of her spiritual and physical aspects. Due to her relaxed, balanced demeanour, though, Skunk is often taken advantage of. She gives freely and unconditionally, usually receiving all the thanks she needs from the look of joy on the faces of those receiving her assistance, support and benefit.

If Skunk has wandered casually into your cards today, you're being warned that if you keep giving of yourself too freely that others will grow to expect it and begin taking your good nature for granted. The problem is, like the Skunk, you probably dislike confrontation and rely heavily on your patience to get you through annoying times. But, like the Skunk, when you find yourself backed into a corner with your emotional buttons being unduly pushed, you know you have the potential to 'explode', retaliating in a forceful way. While you do everything in your control to avoid such outbursts, you sometimes feel as though you're powerless to avoid them. People (and other animals) who find themselves on the receiving end of a Skunk's anger, quickly realise the error of their ways and usually find themselves needing quality time to recover from the experience, with apologies and attempts to explain doing little to ease the Skunk's feelings of frustration and contempt. Skunk demands that when we give from the heart, we do so intermittently to avoid others taking it for granted. Skunk asks if you'd like to remain in a situation that will see you forever walking on eggshells, or is it time to take control of your life while she helps you reinstate a sense of personal power and healthy self-esteem?

CROCODILE
CREATIVE FORCE

The Crocodile is a largely aquatic reptile that rests during the heat of the day in the cool mud of the riverbank. Rich and fertile in nature, mud is symbolic of the blood of the Earth Mother's womb and is associated with the feminine principles of birth, life, death and rebirth. Man observed woman's cycles and made the connection that their blood was somehow connected to conception and the birth of babies. As an emissary of the Earth Mother's blood, therefore, the Crocodile is also a symbol of the creative forces of the world. Crocodile is capable of delivering both tenderness and annihilation. The female Crocodile, for example, is quite capable of brutally killing a mature Buffalo. Alternatively, it tenderly carries her hatchlings from their nest to safety in her powerful jaws. According to Crocodile, death and birth are both vital stages of initiation and she primes us to close one door so that another may open.

If Crocodile has stormed into your cards today you're being reminded to be both gentle and loving even as you're acting hard-nosed and strong. You honour both qualities, but rarely combine the two. You, like the Crocodile, take immediate and steadfast responsibility for all aspects of your life and never feel squeamish about doing what it takes to honour the process. You probably grew up being shown very little encouragement and were frequently forced to fend for yourself and seek emotional nourishment from whoever was willing to offer it. Crocodile people are powerfully creative; a by-product of being forced to think outside the box in order to survive and can turn any negative experience into a positive one. Because of your dogged determination and ruthless nature, you tend to push people away. As a land-dwelling animal and an aquatic one, Crocodile acts as a doorkeeper to the tangible world and the Underworld; the embodiment of both life and death in their purest forms. Crocodile, with its eyes positioned on the top of its head, is asking you to see above and beyond physical limitations and emotional burdens so that we may trust your intuition and manifest your heart's desire.

WEST / WATER
DARK BLUE

HIPPOPOTAMUS
VOLATILITY

Hippopotamus is a Greek word meaning 'River Horse'. Forced to spend much of its daylight hours submerged because its skin loses moisture at an alarming rate when exposed to the air, the Hippopotamus will nibble on aquatic plants while 'floating' with only its eyes and nostrils exposed above the waterline. Loafing on the river banks in a deceptively mild-mannered manner, the Hippopotamus is responsible for the bulk of animal-related human deaths in Africa. Gathering together in groups of up to 150 individuals and opting to graze at night to avoid the sun, Hippopotamuses regularly play-fight to establish and maintain hierarchy, but when provoked, the males will fight to the death.

If the Hippopotamus has floated from the river into your cards today, you're being asked to dive deep to realise the strength to say 'no more' after years of abuse or oppression. Those of us who live a life of pretence, forced silence or persecution are like the submerged Hippopotamus: calmly drifting through the cool waters of a seemingly unsympathetic and perilous environment, interacting effectively with our friends and family while going through the motions of a 'normal' life. However, we're more often than not steaming internally like a volcano on the verge of an emotional eruption. Hippopotamus has come offering you a voice, especially if you have found yourself silenced by external forces until now. Preferring that we seek help by putting a little trust in others, speak up about what's been going on in our world, and that we do what we can to regain some degree of Personal Power (instead of constantly and willingly giving it away), Hippopotamus rejects victim mentality and the overindulgence of the negative 'prostitute' archetype found innately within each of us. So, instead of biting your tongue and suppressing who and what you truly desire at the risk of exploding in a volatile release of pent-up emotion, Hippopotamus says 'Remember that you have a voice and that you are totally equal to everyone around you. Without your input, the world would be less than perfect'.

GIRAFFE
INTERSECTION

The Giraffe is considered to be a sacred vehicle of supernatural power. It symbolises the interconnecting relationship that inherently links the Physical Plane, the Underworld and the Spiritual Realms. Like a tree, the Giraffe stands in all three worlds simultaneously, offering acumen ingrained with sacred experience. An emblematic intersection or 'cross over' point between the worlds, the Giraffe offers choice and understanding to those who seek its wisdom. Offering insight into death, grief, fear, pain, and healing, Giraffe's feet suggest the need to explore the past, to make well all wounds and to productively explore our Inner Landscape while maintaining a strong foothold on reality. Giraffe's torso reminds us to remain practical, strive for realistic goals and productively process the mundane aspects of everyday life offering buoyancy, grounding and stability. The head of the Giraffe, as it probes the heavens, browsing the branches of the tallest trees, offers permission to explore the world's religions and spiritual paths, and to develop our own individual sacred gifts. No matter what the source, Giraffe seeks to introduce us to an aspect of Spirit/God that delivers us back to a place of inner peace, totality and good health.

If the Giraffe has leaned down to peer at your cards, you are being encouraged to explore the great cycle that is life. You are being invited to embark on a journey that will take you to each of the three worlds and embrace what unfolds for you there. Each time you are lost, confused, find yourself in doubt, depressed, or meditating, you are visiting the Underworld. When you find yourself busy with everyday duties, preoccupied by material acquisition, striving for advancement in your chosen area of employ, bettering yourself academically or concentrating on any aspect of routine life, you are working within the physical borders of life. To venture further with your exploration of life, however, and to wonder about what makes the Universe tick, what happens after death, or to ask 'Why am I here?' is to browse the spiritual realms. Giraffe gives you permission to question, to agree or to disagree when it comes to understanding all areas of your life. To figure out which realm you are exploring at present, simply close your eyes, find the inner silence and ask to be directed to one of the Giraffe's three indicators: its feet/legs, torso/shoulders or neck/head.

ASIATIC BLACK BEAR
THE PROSTITUTE

An animal that symbolically sits in the West on the great Wheel of Life, Bears (generically) invite us to ponder life, to seek sacred silence and to meditatively journey deep within so that we might better appreciate our inner awareness. As we watch the moon grow in size and power, though, the Asiatic Black (or 'Moon' Bear more specifically) prompts us to seek and trust the answers we may find deep within our inner knowing before we go seeking the wisdom of others. Moon Bear invites us to stand contemplatively, facing the sun as it sets, all the while asking for the opportunity to reflect, to be calm and to self-asses. We treat the Moon Bear (and many other aspects of Nature) with indifference: as a tool, as an easily discarded implement to be used and abused for our pleasure and personal gain. We may protect and love the Moon Bear, but then we ignore the breaking of this pact because it is easier to do than honour the changes that need to be made, changes that will productively affect the bigger picture. We would rather turn a blind eye and sell ourselves short, than speak up and put things right.

With Moon Bear ambling reflectively into your cards today, the inherent prostitute that exists within all of us is being reflected back at you: that part of yourself that is willing to compromise your mind, body and spirit in order to feel whole, better or worthy. It represents the shadow-side tendency to sell yourself short, to sell yourself out, to reject personal values and morals and to ignore sanctified beliefs in order to gain or maintain a sense of security, support, relationship or approval. It allows you to make excuses for your actions. Moon Bear demonstrates the futility of believing the self-styled facades and lies we hide behind in order to avoid taking responsibility for our actions and reactions. It represents the fabricated, manipulated and self-serving beliefs that bind us, essentially holding our soul ransom. If Moon Bear has made its way into your cards today, you're being asked to take down the figurative 'for sale sign' that has presented your sacred self to the highest bidder for years, and to no longer believe that 'everything (and everyone) has a price'. Some things are priceless and cannot be replaced.

GIANT PANDA
SORROW

There is a Chinese legend that tells how the Giant Panda came to have black-and-white fur. A little girl was walking through the forest when she came across a Leopard and a White Panda engaged in battle. The girl grabbed the Leopard's tail and tried to drag him away. The Leopard reacted by killing her instantly. The Panda turned on its heels and fled into the forest. When the Panda heard later that the little girl had died, he was distraught. During the funeral the Pandas became so distressed that they began to cry. They cried so much that when they dabbed their eyes with the black arm bands they wore in her honour, the colour in the arm bands bled, staining their legs and paws black. As they dabbed their eyes, they became black also. They hugged one another and left black bands around their waists, and to block out the sounds of the crying Pandas, put their paws over their ears, turning them black too. Legend explains the Giant Pandas decided to keep their black-and-white markings in honour of the selfless little girl.

If Giant Panda has ambled into your cards today, you're being reminded how compassionate, empathetic and sensitive to the suffering of others you are. There's little doubt that you weep tears of remorse when you hear news reports of beached Whales, natural disasters and plane crashes and you feel you should be doing more, with no idea of how to go about doing it. Knowing this, Giant Panda has come to encourage you to embrace a deeper understanding and reflective approach to helping others reclaim clarity. You need to find a gentle way to distance yourself from the emotional circumstances of others in order to see and appreciate why things happen and what needs to be done to bring about positive change. Giant Panda warns, however, of becoming too involved in how others may choose to process change and to avoid becoming personally affected by its conclusion. Otherwise you run the risk of burning yourself out or breaking down emotionally beneath the burden of guilt and sadness you carry on behalf of the world. Giant Panda encourages you to 'cry for the people' as a viable and sacred medicine, but not at the expense of your own emotional state. Giant Panda will always be your support, especially when you value your personal wellbeing equally as that of those around you.

RED PANDA
COMPASSION

Sharing the humble, modest and empathetic energy of the Giant Panda, the Red Panda is said to resonate to the energy of Quan Yin, the goddess of compassion and mercy. The Red Panda hears and responds to the cry of all beings. Comfortable with its emotions and unafraid to show them, the Red Panda strengthens courage, enhances creativity and offers a keen and rapid force that brings light into our life and illuminates our path. Red Panda stimulates, quickens and transforms all who are drawn to explore it, while affording enlightened spirituality, wisdom, strength and the divine power of personal transformation. Quan Yin is said to have promised the people that she would not return to Heaven until all living things had discovered and honoured their purpose, while the Red Panda sits midpoint between Heaven and Earth, perched high in the trees, looking down compassionately upon the people.

If Red Panda is humbly sitting among your cards today, it's probably because you find it hard to punish, blame or accuse anyone because your heart is free of vengeance and self-importance. Although ever watchful, Red Panda has turned up today to inspire you to grow and heal. It comes promising to fill you with an overwhelming sense of empathy whenever you lose sight of your own divinity and connection to Spirit, and to remind you of the sacredness found in all life and the inherent relationship you share with the world around you. Red Panda's energy will eventually deliver you from a place of ego into a state of humility and gratitude whenever you find yourself taking things for granted or when you've forgotten to show appreciation for the beauty in your life. So, if Red Panda has appeared in your cards, it's time to nurture and integrate the beauty and compassion of Quan Yin into your life, while encouraging others to integrate it into theirs. If you yearn to see the world become a better place, with Red Panda's help you will make your yearning a reality.

BLACK BEAR
INTROSPECTION

The Black Bear is a wise, meditative fellow who would rather listen to his own counsel than seek that of another. He encourages us to follow suit; to silence the inner chatter, to sit in silent contemplation and to find the answers we seek within the solitude of our own mind. The Bear's cave represents the womb of the Earth Mother and the wisdom stored deep within the subconscious mind. As such, the cave is a symbol of growth, with the act of entering being a return to the centre of the sacred self, a 'death' of sorts, and our emergence signifying the act of rebirth. Black Bear teaches us to release that which no longer serves us, thus making way for new beginnings. The Black Bear may appear aloof but in reality, because of an inherent sensitivity to the world around them, they are simply filtering and integrating what their conscious mind is showing them to be real in relation to what their subconscious instinctively is reminding them of what they KNOW to be true.

If Black Bear sits pondering your cards with you today, you're probably being encouraged to spend time alone, reflecting on how very creative and profoundly visual you. You are being encouraged to remember how self-sufficient and powerfully intuitive you are, and how you need to pay heed to your own personal values and beliefs instead of relying on those of your family and friends so much. Black Bear asks that you begin to nurture a greater appreciation for silence, solitude, meditation, prayer and positive change, by better understanding the principles of introspection, death and rebirth. By calling upon the Black Bear, there's also a very good chance that you have a predilection for astral travel, lucid dreaming and mystical growth and development of any kind. Black Bear is the totem of healers, teachers and dream interpreters, for the Black Bear is the keeper of Inner Knowing. So, if the Black Bear has wandered into your cards, embrace his wisdom, you will finally break through the illusions of personal limitation and false belief and realise a willingness to step into the unknown. Black Bear is asking you to ponder life, contemplate your ultimate spiritual path and make productive, self-empowering, goal-achieving choices. If you do, your quality of life will surely improve.

CROW
LAW

Flying together in flocks known as 'murders', the Crow is a messenger of a mystical place known as the 'Black Lodge', or the 'Lodge of Women'. The 'Lodge of Women' is likened to the Void; the Universal Womb, the source of all understanding, inspiration and knowing. As a creature of the Void, Crow exists in the past, present and future simultaneously, perceiving the darkness within light and the light within darkness while seeing all worlds and dimensions from every vantage point. Governed by an unprecedented understanding of Universal law, Crow speaks of truth and wisdom unheard of in any human law system. When we call to Spirit for help we invite change and

Crow promises to deliver the change. It is not unusual, therefore, for this change to be hidden within some devastating incident or traumatic experience. When we honour the ways of Crow and strive to live by the laws determined by Creation, the reward is that we are allowed to leave this world and move to the next with clear memory of our previous life experiences.

If Crow stands solicitously in your cards today, you are being reminded of your responsibility to your thoughts and reasons, and your ability to reinstate clarity in the minds of those around you. Crow is reminding you to walk in beauty within yourself, to live your truth, to find your purpose and to live it, without question or doubt. It comes heralding a journey into your past to consider the lessons you experienced there, remaining fully in the present at the same time. In doing so, you will find the strength and the wisdom to walk into your future, free of shadows and doubt. By breathing life into your future, you will begin to see your messages from Spirit becoming reality because you are positively shape-shifting your consciousness. Crow foresees the realisation of true love, healthy emotions, developing intuition and sacred intimacy. But she can do so by first checking that you have done what's required to welcome them into your life. If, for example, you know there are things you need to deal with and you begin the process of healing, but you shy away at the last moment, be warned; Crow will assume you have decided not to honour your end of the bargain and will symbolically slam down the judicial hammer. Put simply, if you choose to sit in denial and refuse to acknowledge your responsibilities willingly, then she will force you to step into the light of realisation, by delivering you first into a time of extreme darkness from which light will slowly begin to emerge.

DOLPHIN BREATH

Witnessing the joyful behaviour of a Dolphin at play, anyone would agree that they are beautiful and awe-inspiring. What's more awe-inspiring is the knowing that the Dolphin has energetically been with us from birth as a protector, guide and teacher. As we've journeyed though life, Dolphin has swam by our side, checking constantly to ensure that every breath we take is rich with self-respect and purpose. Dolphin welcomes Spirit into our heart and mind by breathing life into the light that resides in each of us. During childbirth, expectant mothers are told to 'breathe' their way through the pain and rush of emotion. In our mother's womb we exist in a safe world and the slightest hint of stress during this time will quickly result in our mother's heart-rate rising. We then feel our heart-rate rise to match that of our mother's. As our mother's heartbeat returns to its normal rate, so will ours. We quickly learn to adapt to the constant nervous energy that dominates the fluid in which we live and, when we are born, we sometimes retain that. Realising what life was like for both you and your mother while she was carrying you will help you understand why you may hold your breath in times of stress.

If Dolphin has swam into your cards today, you're being reminded of the fact that Dolphin has been with you since you signed your sacred contract long before your birth; a contract that outlines every aspect of your Earth. Spirit does not make mistakes and neither do you, and Dolphin supports the life we have chosen. She is encouraging you to revisit your sacred breath each time you conceive of and 'birth' new ideas, create new things or embark on new relationships. Breath is life, Dolphin is asking you to review it by asking yourself and your family questions surrounding your time spent in the womb and to consider the possibility that there may be aspects of your life that may be hindered or hampered by your memory of your time there. Dolphin remains with you always; offering support and protection, inspiring your dreams, desires and aspirations until called upon to help you plot your course back to Spirit. To honour Dolphin is to know that the first breath you took was healthy and strong, and that the last one you take is more of a sigh … one that confirms contentment with your efforts and achievements during life; a sigh that ensures the first breaths taken by generations to come are those of abundance, interconnectedness and good health. Dolphin is asking you to just slow down and breathe.

JAGUAR IMPECCABILITY

The Black Jaguar (also known as the Black 'Panther') is simply a regular Jaguar displaying the melanistic gene evident in most Cats. The Black Jaguar is a 'yin' animal, which means it's a lunar-influenced creature, feminine in nature and ruled by water and nurtures us through change, death, the evolution of the soul and embracing of the unknown. The 'regular' Jaguar (as a solar-influenced creature; an emissary of fire, the masculine principles and action), sheds light on death, so that we may fear it less. Jaguar teaches us that death is best seen as a process that inspires deeper understanding of change and transformation. When death occurs, it offers a chance to surrender to the

Void; a chance to openly grieve for the wrongs that have been inflicted upon us; a chance to scream at the Universe and ask 'Why'? Death is always pre-destined, agreed to by all parties prior. Death forces us to step out and appreciate life and to live ours closer to Spirit. In doing so, we make a vow to avenge the death; to make it mean something. When we honour this vow, we inherently embrace and honour the reason for the death in the first place. We subconsciously remember the agreement that person made with us before we entered the Earth-plane. To not honour our spiritual destiny, is to dishonour the vow. Such a promise is made with the understanding that our grief is what fuels the fire and breathes life into the quest and gives the journey purpose.

If Jaguar has stepped solemnly into your cards today, you're being offered the chance to embrace the unknown and explore the Void. You are being urged to only ask questions that you're prepared to receive and hear the answers to, and to honourably heed and honour how you respond to them. Jaguar teaches us to walk the Warrior's Path to freedom and to embrace 'death' in its many guises with faith and integrity. It asks that you demonstrate impeccable self-respect by walking in truth, the whole time honouring the life you live in the hope that you demonstrate unwavering commitment to the vows you made before entering the Earth-plane. Jaguar asks that you both speak and live your truth, and value your integrity above all else.

SPIDER
THE WEAVER

According to Native American folklore, it was Grandmother Spider who sang the Universe into being by weaving the Web of Life. Grandmother Spider wove the first Dream Catcher. In the centre she placed a single turquoise stone, a symbol of connection to the Creative Force, of clarity, peace, communication and protection. With the aid of the Dream Catcher, Spider says our dreams can be harnessed and fruitfully brought to fruition. Spider is the weaver of visions. She helps us remember that we hold our destiny in the palm of our hand. As such, we are the creators of our own lives, solely responsible for the choices we make. Spider reassures us that if we do not like what we are offered in life, we can return to the centre of the Web and choose for ourselves. We each form a vital strand in the Web of Life. Without our productive input, the Web's integrity is breached thus causing confusion and stagnation in our life. We are encouraged to explore life, to investigate all the strands on offer and to make the most of them. The Web of Life is riddled with pitfalls, but it also promises greatness to those prepared to take risks and to work hard.

If Spider has woven her way into your cards today, she is offering to help reweave your web when your path seems empty and unrewarding. Spider wants you to reclaim your power and to bring your dreams to fruition. She asks that you remember that in order to open new doors you must first close old ones, face all your fears and make choices that will create opportunity for new beginnings. Spider has appeared today to remind you of the sacred role you play as a vital strand in the Web of Life. She knows that you yearn to take control of your life and to make a difference in the world, to believe in yourself, to have faith in your ability to heal and to realise your true potential. So by dropping into your cards today, it is clear that Spider wants you to realise the healing wisdom that resides deep within your being that's capable of making your life rich and rewarding and powerfully so.

WHALE
GROUND SIGNATURES

Whale stores the Earth Mother's sacred records and pays witness to the proceedings that collectively authenticate the spiritual makeup of the planet by holding the memories of each and every event that has ever contributed to her shaping. She channels this information to our subconscious mind through our dreams, visions and ponderings so that we may remember our spiritual history and the sacred places that have shaped our personal journey. It is believed that those who work with Whale hold within their DNA the ability to hear the secret language encoded in the audible rhythms and vibrations generated by the Earth Mother. The Whale's song offers us the chance to reconnect with the heartbeat and ground signature of Mother Earth. The more we judge and repress others, lie, manipulate, cheat and steal, the more we rape the planet and take that which is not rightfully ours, the greater the gap we build between our healing and that of the Earth Mother. Could this be why Whales beach themselves? If so, perhaps they are trying to wake us up before the Earth Mother gives up. So, let's make a pact to begin today. Make peace where petty unrest lies, say sorry and appreciate the little things while rejecting greed, fear and prejudice.

If the Whale has sung its way into your cards today, you're being asked to embrace how sensitive you are to your environment and realise how your strong, psychic connection to the Earth Mother may affect your life. Whale realises that you need stable surroundings and reliable relationships to maintain an overall sense of wellbeing. Without these things, you tend to experience mood swings and emotional periods. If you find yourself feeling; aggressive just before an electrical storm, depressed after extended periods of rain and overly energetic during sunny weather, then Whale is correct in her assessment of you and your relationship to the Earth Mother. She has affirmed your sensitivity to the vibrations, or 'ground signatures', emitted by the Earth Mother. The more you learn to surrender to the ebb and flow that is the Earth Mother's way you will find yourself not only falling gently in line with her rhythm, but more passionately into your own inner rhythm and, in time, that of those who share your world.

SOUTH / EARTH
LEAF GREEN

AFRICAN ELEPHANT
COMMITMENT

Weighing in at over 6000 kilograms as an adult, the African Elephant has longer tusks and larger ears than its Asian cousin and has been known to live up to 65 years in the wild. It is not uncommon for remains of a deceased loved one to be visited year after year, with time taken by those still living to 'cry' before moving on. Relationships between group members are tight, with each member honoured for their individual strengths and it is the oldest non-reproducing females that lead the herd because of their extensive knowledge and wisdom. According to many folk stories, the African Elephant's wisdom was regularly sought out by the animals who saw it as a spiritual messenger and sacred oracle; a wise chief who, without bias, settled disputes among the other animals.

If African Elephant has treaded softly into your cards today, you are being reminded of the commitment you made at birth to honour your family (whatever 'family' means to you) and your community. You are also being asked to consider the promises you've made to others and those that have been made to you. Due to its enduring memory, loyalty and sense of obligation, African Elephant awakens a sense of duty to the promises we've made and the commitments we have forged by instilling a greater sense of responsibility. To have the African Elephant pay you a visit today, you may find illusions being shattered and truths being revealed, especially illusions of security and commitment created by assumptions on your part; unspoken contracts you assumed were in place but were never actualised and it's here that the trauma of realisation hits. The African Elephant is the true friend of children of broken families, those enduring marriage breakdowns, unexpected redundancies or the death of a loved one and anyone who finds themselves feeling betrayed or forsaken. When you invoke the African Elephant, you're establishing a powerful sense of commitment to yourself, those that you love and, in truth, your own self-worth.

OSTRICH GROUNDING

The flightless Ostrich is the largest living bird on earth. Male Ostriches have black feathers on their back and white primary feathers on their wings and tail. Females and young Ostriches have brown feathers (instead of black) to offer camouflage and protection against predators. Only about 15% of Ostrich chicks survive their first year, with many of them falling prey to Vultures, Hyenas and Jackals. Ostriches usually choose to live alone, but will occasionally travel in loose flocks. Living for 40 years or more, Ostriches are gifted with powerful vision and agility. Because Ostriches do not have teeth, they swallow pebbles that grind their food in their gizzard and can carry as much as one kilogram (2.2

lb) of stones in their stomachs. Equipped with well-developed leg muscles, Ostriches can reach speeds of up to 30 miles (just over 48 kilometres) per hour, but contrary to folklore, they do not bury their heads in the sand.

If the Ostrich stands tall and proud in your cards today, you're being encouraged to ground your energy by imagining your pockets filled with heavy stones, and to nurture yourself instead of drifting aimlessly through life. Ostrich is an animal that only accepts black or white answers. It's not one to compromise or to recognise 'shades of grey'. When it asks a question, it only accepts a straight 'yes' or 'no' response. If Ostrich has appeared today, you're being asked to stand firmly by your convictions and to never consider retreat unless hopelessly backed up against a wall. The Ostrich abhors cowardice and gutless behaviour. To be held accountable for the affect you have on others is the keynote message of the Ostrich, as is the importance of self-respect. It is important at this time to maintain eye contact with everyone you meet, display relaxed body language and only ever engage in meaningful conversation. By honouring yourself and building self-respect, you heighten your awareness of others. By living your life in a responsible manner, you will soon find yourself attracting people of similar vibration. In short, you are being encouraged to take a practical stance, to ground your otherwise flighty attitude and behaviour and take responsibility for all areas of your life. Don't deny anyone or anything, especially when you know you are accountable, and always 'Walk your Talk'.

CHIMPANZEE ASCENSION

Believed to be the closest relative or man, Chimpanzees can live for more than 50 years. They are famous for their use of tools, such as sticks to extract Termites from their mounds. Threatened by loss of habitat and poaching, Chimpanzees lead a very structured life with signals, verbal demonstrations and 'language' ascertaining the community standing of an individual. The Swahili word for Chimpanzee is *ki-mpanzi*, which means 'little climber'. Some Indigenous people of Africa's rainforest regions honour them as protectors of the people and even as messengers of the gods. Local legend tells of a lost hunter who was helped by a Chimpanzee that brought him berries and water.

The pair was spied by a young girl who ran to her father and told him to offer assistance because he must be 'loved by the gods' to have a Chimpanzee as an adviser. The story spread quickly, and the Chimpanzee soon became an emissary of the gods. Those who carry the Chimpanzee in their hearts are thought to be similarly blessed by Spirit and protected by the gods.

If Chimpanzee has climbed into your cards today, embrace the belief that you are worthy of great things because, to have the Chimpanzee decide to willingly walk with you is to know, without question, that the gods are smiling on you at this time. The Chimpanzee card is a sign that you will soon be afforded the opportunity of advancement or the chance to transcend the mundane in some way. As the 'little climber', the Chimpanzee doesn't sit contently on the bottom rung of the ladder for very long. Striving to always ascend and better himself, the Chimpanzee teaches us to view ourselves as unique, talented and set apart from others in a sacred way. If you follow the Chimpanzee's lead, you will find that you cannot fail in your bid to better yourself. You may also find yourself continually being offered opportunities to climb to greater heights, both inwardly and in the physical world. As you climb, you will be offered a powerful vantage point that will help you realise ways to improve yourself and your life. Chimpanzee is asking you to not only work hard, but to rely on your intuition to see clearly into the future because, when you trust and celebrate your relationship with Spirit, you will always do well.

ORANG-UTAN
MAN OF THE FOREST

In Malay, *Orang-utan* means 'Man of the Forest'. Enjoying a largely arboreal life, the Orang-utan has little need to venture down to the forest floor. Sadly, Orang-utans are fast becoming endangered as a species, with wild populations declining almost to the point of extinction. Orang-utans are highly intelligent and have been seen using found objects as tools; covering their baby's heads with leaves to save them getting wet or using sticks to pry open fruit. An animal so dependent on the forest for its survival, it's not difficult to see a contemporary association between the Orang-utan and the ancient 'Green Man' of Celtic folklore. Such beings, of which there are many variants, were once revered as protectors of the forests and the trees and animals that dwelt therein. According to legend, whenever we cut down a tree for reasons other than absolute need, the weaker we render the protective power of the Green Man. And when the final tree is eventually felled, the spirit of the Green Man will die forever. When we ignore the sacredness of life on Earth, we lose sight of our own potential and sense of belonging and with each stroke of the axe we essentially cut our own life-line and connection to one other.

If Orang-utan has gently shuffled into your cards today, you are being asked to speak up in defence of our beautiful planet. To offer a voice for the voiceless by saying, 'Stop everyone! Enough's enough!' Orang-utan instils a sense of awe and respect for the magnificence, power and structured composition of Nature, particularly the world's jungles, forests and woodlands. As the voice and guardian of this untamed beauty, Orang-utan has appeared today to remind you of the sacred role you play in maintaining the wellbeing of the planet. By showing responsibility for your life, how you live it and what you do to make the world a better place, you're teaching by example and demonstrating by doing how others may follow suit. You're showing up the ignorance and nearsightedness of those around you by highlighting how sacred life is by living your life accordingly. You're offering them permission to stop and appreciate the natural world that surrounds them, every moment of every day. You can make miracles happen by raising awareness by simply telling one friend about the plight of the animals, the environment, and the natural world as a whole and inviting them to tell two, in the hope that they will each tell four.

BISON
SACRED PRAYER

It is estimated that close to 60 million American Buffalo or 'Bison' once roamed the Great Plains of North America. Most people have has seen images of Native American Chiefs holding Buffalo skulls high above their heads, a stance that inspires a sense of humility and reverence, a need for sacred silence and connection to Spirit. The skull was seen as a channel for divine communication and a means of gaining insight, guidance and encouragement from Spirit. Buffalo builds on what is regarded as a practical and fruitful life by integrating a meaningful, unified spiritual foundation that offers choice, balance and wholeness. By honouring the sacred, we enhance the mundane. Our chores and tasks, which may normally weigh heavily on our hearts, dulling our sense of purpose, become instead mini celebrations of the divine. To acknowledge Spirit and to welcome it into your life is to know you are not alone. It is to remember and restore Sacred Unity to all aspects of existence.

If Buffalo has reverently made its way into your cards, you're being asked to picture yourself raising your arms, as if in the sacred act of beckoning, and to call from your heart of hearts to the Creator Spirit whenever you feel lost, alone or forsaken. Offer your voice to the Spirits, with the expectation that your words and heart's yearning will be heard. In doing so, you will not only begin to find yourself supported by Spirit, you will also reignite a sense of unity within yourself. You will have initiated the process of 'welcoming yourself home' by acknowledging your inherent relationship to all things. When you call to Spirit, you call to and reconnect with the Spirit or life-force found within all things, you call to the Spirit within yourself. Sacred Unity can only be achieved when you are fully committed to consciously doing what needs to be done to make your life richer and more complete. Enjoying a practical and fruitful life means living, breathing and celebrating your very existence with everything you do. To be supported, for example, you must be prepared to support. To be loved unconditionally, you must be prepared to love unconditionally. But most of all, you must make the conscious decision to reward yourself with the seemingly elusive gift of self-love, and you must make a pact to empower and strengthen this gift each and every day, in everything you do and with every breath you take.

PUMA
LEADERSHIP

The Puma (also known as the Cougar, Catamount or Mountain Lion) is a largely solitary animal that's active during the day and night. With the strength and power to bring down a Horse, Pumas as a whole are more likely to hunt wild Deer, Rabbits, Hare and even Mice. An animal that knows well the gifts of self-direction and sacrifice, the Puma remains true to its heart in everything it does, with a focus on living its life from a place of integrity and honour. As such, the Puma makes for a brave and genuine leader. A true leader: must be respected by their followers if they are to instil a sense of trust and loyalty in others; are best elected by the people; must not be afraid to direct, delegate or take responsibility when no one else is willing to do so; must be prepared to 'take the blame'; must not be swayed by their own inherent biases or uncertainty of others; nor can they allow self-importance influence their decision-making; must immediately see what needs to be done and be strong enough to act accordingly with little or no support; must appear impartial, composed and in control, even when they are inwardly feeling overwhelmed, afraid or confused.

If the Puma has earned a place in your cards today, you are being asked to 'step up' in some area of your life, and to take on a role of leadership. It seems that a person (or people) may need you to take the lead at this time, and you are being invited to demonstrate faith and inner-strength, maturity and wholeness to fulfil that role. While it seems you have little choice but to step into the role, be warned: the path of the true leader is fraught with trial and tribulation; obstacles that will test your resolve, commitment and personal belief. Puma expects that, as a leader, it is time to earn the respect of others instead of expecting it or demanding it. It is time to learn how to show respect and compassion for others, even when you feel they don't deserve it. As a leader you must: demonstrate a love and deep respect for all living things and for Nature as a whole; not only recognise all life as being sacred and deserving of respect, but you must also find a way of demonstrating it so that others will want to follow suit; consider the ways of the Universe and the wants and needs of others before you even begin to contemplate your own. Now that you have been recognised as a worthy leader, you may find that people look to you differently. And while this may only be a perception based on low self-esteem or self-worth, there's bound to be an element of sacred truth to it. Puma is asking you to step up and to follow your purpose. It's like you've been issued a spiritual directive to inspire others to reach a unified goal. And here is the warning issued earlier: you must guard against becoming a 'guru', one who has 'devotees' rather than simple followers. Such a step is an impertinent blight against the message of the Puma, and one that is sure to see you stumble and fall.

DOG
LOYALTY

Dogs have lived and worked in close proximity with man since the beginning of time it seems, so much so that their loyalty has earned them the title of 'man's best friend'. Those that know Dog understand without question that they personify love, the true essence of Spirit. Without love, there is no sense of promise, no purpose, no light, no reason to look forward and no opportunity to embrace new beginnings. By its very nature, Dog encourages us to celebrate love, to live life to the fullest and to relish in those we hold dear. It's not uncommon for people to sometimes question the love they have for their spouses, partners or companions or feel as though their relationships are mostly one-sided. And it's actually normal for people to occasionally find reason to question their partner's commitment and loyalty. It's normal too, for people to forget to ponder the flipside to this question; to fail to consider that perhaps their partner is worrying about the health of their relationship or feeling the same way about them. Dog believes the best way to show our feelings is to action them. When doubt is plaguing your mind, for example, reassuring words, even if said from the heart, may help to alleviate our fears, actions fuelled by passion and commitment hold the power to put them to rest forever. Being told, 'I love you', for example, is a beautiful thing, but nothing anchors the sentiment more profoundly than an act of love. Actioning your love will not only secure belief in its existence in your partner's consciousness forever, but it will also mirror the joy it inspires back at you.

If the Hound has lurched joyfully into your cards today, you're being encouraged to celebrate love and to live your life to the fullest. Due to its inherent sense of loyalty, Dog embodies the purest example of unconditional love, faith and tolerance. To treat a Dog with respect and commitment will see the animal return its love, devotion and loyalty tenfold. You're being asked to make it your mission, to learn forgiveness, if not for someone else, then perhaps for yourself. It's time to learn tolerance and to perhaps accept the imperfections you see in others and to view these as mirrors of your own flaws. If Dog has appeared in your cards, it's time to not only appreciate the loyalty you see in others, but to direct a little self-loyalty your own way. A pack-oriented creature, the Dog teaches us to understand boundaries and order within our family and broader community by demonstrating faith in its own beliefs and values. Dog appreciates that it's often necessary to consider the needs of the pack as a whole first and to never become so submissive to the wants and desires of others that we lose our own identity and sense of integrity. Dog is a powerful teacher and asks that you trust, love and accept: qualities that can only be found in others when you first realise them within yourself.

RABBIT
FERTILITY

The Rabbit in its many guises is an animal that's preyed upon by most of, if not all, the world's predatory species. Nature has compensated the Rabbit by gifting it with an almost unbridled fertility rate: a single female can produce as many as 30 offspring a year. Rabbit embodies Mother Nature's ever-changing cycles: growth; life, death and rebirth. Symbolic of seasonal change, of new life in the spring, energy and vitality in summer; the inward contemplation of autumn and the wisdom and maturity of winter; to yet again return to the rebirth of spring, Rabbit keeps us in touch with the great circle of life and the natural harmony found between and within everything of Nature. When we acknowledge our relationship to all things, the Web of Life is honoured and balance is restored. To give to the Earth Mother by walking with her, instead of simply on her, our quality of life deepens, with all ventures embarked upon prospering beyond our wildest dreams.

If Rabbit has hopped into your cards today, you're being reminded to walk gently upon the Earth, with a sense of reverence for and honour of all things. To do so will see your wants and needs supported by Spirit and your life become more fertile, abundant and free of obstacles. Rabbit helps us notice Nature's portents and the cycles of change within ourselves. When you walk in harmony with the world around you, you can't help but become one with it. The greater the love and encouragement you afford it, the more you will be rewarded. Rabbit is encouraging you to view your body as a sacred temple, a representation of Spirit and a way of acknowledging the miracle of life. Take notice of the subtle internal changes that will take place when you begin to walk hand in hand with Nature, because they will be plentiful. Your love for your friends and family will become richer, your self-respect will flourish, and your ability to create will demand to be recognised. Rabbit ensures that your life is soon to become richer, brighter and more meaningful, especially when you back it up with dedication, empathy, passion and a sense of sacredness.

JACKAL
DEATH

Anubis was a canine-headed, pointy-eared funerary deity of ancient Egypt and it's fairly well-established as a belief that Anubis was most likely inspired by the Jackal and was responsible for guiding the dead deep into the Underworld where their souls would be judged and perhaps offered eternal life. As such, the Jackal helps us view change in its many guises as being symbolic of death; a ritualistic process that sees the familiar aspects of the self surrendered in favour of a new phase. Jackal teaches us to welcome necessary change, healthy endings and closure of any kind as opportunities to rebirth our true self over and over again. Relationships that no longer nurture the soul, jobs that no longer stimulate the mind and spirit and homes that have become houses can all be honourably put to rest by calling upon the wisdom of the Jackal.

If Jackal has wandered solemnly into your cards today, see it as a sign that it's time to bring closure to a 'dead' area of your life. In the process of letting go, though, remember to hold truth and integrity as your highest priority so that if other people are involved, they will also receive the blessing of your decision to let go or cease control. Your intent to bring about change must weigh pure. If you fail to demonstrate impeccability in all your dealings, Jackal will deny all knowledge and abandon you in your efforts. If greed, jealousy or revenge is what motivates your desire for change or endings, then beware the consequences. If Jackal has chosen to appear in your cards today, perhaps it's more than just change that you're experiencing, but an actual death or the physical passing of a loved one or friend. Jackal has therefore chosen to materialise as an offering to guide your dearly departed to the Afterlife. Rest assured that the Jackal has also come to offer understanding, reason, comfort and peace to those left behind. Working with the Jackal and learning to understand its wisdom may see you become a powerful mediator. It's a sign that you are being acknowledged as a purifier and cleaner of sorts and proof that you're an honourable, hardworking and trustworthy person, humble enough to willingly do what others may deem distasteful or difficult to stomach. So hold your head up and see yourself as a person of high integrity, because that's how the Jackal views you.

TURKEY
SHARED BLESSINGS

Synonymous with Thanksgiving, the Turkey has become an emissary of autumn and the harvest. The Aztecs once cast solid-gold ornaments of the bird to use as offerings of thanks to the gods. Although capable of flight, the Turkey is a bird of the Earth. Also known as the Ground Eagle, the Turkey is an emblem of the spiritual wisdom radiated by the Earth Mother and the shared blessings she offers. Her blessings come in the form of her gifts: plentiful crops, healing herbs, minerals, timber, water and animals. Turkey encourages us to use these blessings well and to give thanks and give back to the Earth Mother. Acknowledging the sacrifices made by another is the Turkey's strength, which readily gives of itself so that others may prosper. The Turkey honours the 'giveaway': a traditional ritual that sees the giving away of what you have in excess to those who have little. Turkey gives of itself to exchange life for death. It sacrifices itself to feed others, honour their lives and strengthen their bond with Spirit and the Earth Mother.

If the Turkey has strutted its way into your cards today, you're being asked to divide your bounty, or give something away for the sake of seeing the joy on the face of another. Seeing someone smile can make us feel good, especially when the smile is the result of something we have done for them. A very special thing to do is to share something that is important to you with someone who is having a hard time, or to give a favourite thing away that you don't use anymore. Your favourite thing may become their favourite thing, forging a bond of fondness that can never be broken. To give something away because you know it will make someone feel good is the way of the Turkey. Giving something away can be as simple as offering someone a little of your time or your support. A little of your lunch can ease the pang of hunger in another's stomach, while a friendly smile can mean a lot to someone who feels alone. Turkey reminds you that the more you give of yourself, the more the world will want to share with you.

MOOSE
DURABILITY

The Moose is the largest member of the Deer family. It is a land-dwelling animal that feeds primarily on waterweed and aquatic plant-life. The Moose has become a symbol of wisdom, strength and stamina for the People of North America. Those who yearn for stability and emotional balance may look to the Moose for reassurance. According to legend, the Moose was said to suffer from the 'falling-sickness' (epilepsy) and to combat its unsettling side effects, it would place its left rear hoof in its left ear. To invoke Moose is to offer permanent relief from the ailment. When I first met my wife she suffered from what was first believed to be epilepsy. It turned out she suffered from what was once known as 'hysteria'; a condition where someone temporarily loses all sense of willpower due to a flood of crushing fear or stress triggered by the recollection of past traumatic events. I drew a Moose and, as I drew, silently invoked the spirit of the Moose, asking the whole time for help to relieve the symptoms. After framing the drawing, I gifted it to her, explaining its significance and more than 15 years on, my wife has not had an attack since.

If Moose has purposefully walked into your cards today, you're being asked to embrace your emotional self and to see it as your ally and friend. Instead of seeing yourself as someone ruled by your fears and emotions, begin to celebrate your sensitivities as a gift. The Moose is often seen walking with the dreamers and visionaries among us, and there's a huge chance that you are one too. While allowing people like you to gain sustenance from their emotions and to channel their intuitive selves effectively, the Moose simultaneously offers them grounding and stability. If the Moose has appeared in your cards, see it as a sign that you have a strong inner knowing but be aware that you may allow fear and confusion to rule you, with your gut feeling and mental processes constantly locking horns. Moose asks that you navigate yourself through the emotional pool of life in a practical, grounded manner. While gaining sustenance through emotional nourishment, the Moose will support you if you're prepared to take responsibility for your life and show accountability for your decisions and your actions. In exchange, Moose will see you marry your need for permanence and your inherent sense of vulnerability with everlasting confidence and grounding.

There comes a time in our life when we realise that, at some point on our life journey, we seem to have 'wandered off the path'. *Earth Mother Dreaming* recounts Scott Alexander King's journey from the world of detachment and anger to the world of truth, purity and enlightenment.

Earth Mother Dreaming is an encyclopaedia of all things metaphysical that includes simple yet practical and effective activities, rituals and ceremonies that will see you slowly emerge back into a place of personal power and passion.

- Cleanse and empower your aura and chakras.
- Learn about prayers of smoke, the power of the four directions, smudging, vision quest and the medicine walk.
- Explore the realm of faerie.
- Discover how to make a medicine pouch, medicine shield, dream catcher and journey drum.
- Find out how to give thanks, surrender to Spirit, and how to access your totems and spirit helpers.
- Journey through the wheel of life and realise your personal gifts of power by participating in sacred dance, breath, song and divination while learning how to follow the omens, signs and portents of nature.

ISBN: 9781921878534

Available in all good bookstores and online at
www.rockpoolpublishing.com.au